"Then **Bavaro** Said to **Simms...**"

The Best New York Giants Stories Ever Told

Steve Zipay

D0596989

TRIUMPH
B O O K S

Library of Congress Cataloging-in-Publication Data

Zipay, Steve, 1952–
    Then Bavaro said to Simms—: the best New York Giants stories ever told / Steve Zipay.
        p. cm.
ISBN 978-1-60078-271-8
1. New York Giants (Football team)—History. I. Title.
GV956.N4Z57 2009
796.332'64097471—dc22

                                                           2009017623

This book is available in quantity at special discounts for your group or organization. For further information, contact:

Triumph Books
542 South Dearborn Street
Suite 750
Chicago, Illinois 60605
(312) 939-3330
Fax (312) 663-3557
www.triumphbooks.com

Printed in U.S.A.
ISBN: 978-1-60078-271-8
Design by Patricia Frey
Editorial and page production by Prologue Publishing Services, LLC
Photos courtesy of AP Images except where otherwise indicated

To Laura and Marisa, forever my fair ladies

table of
contents

chapter 1

A Giant Upset: The Miraculous 2007 Season

An Inauspicious Beginning

A summer storm rumbled over the New York Giants' training camp in Albany, New York, in the early-morning hours of July 28, 2007, dampening the practice plans of head coach Tom Coughlin.

The Giants had finished a disappointing 8–8 the previous season, and clouds already had been forming over this one as well: multitalented running back Tiki Barber had retired, and on the way to his television career, sharply criticized Coughlin's strict protocol and all-business demeanor. Star defensive lineman Michael Strahan was holding out for a contract and was undecided on whether to play another year. Veteran wide receiver Amani Toomer was recovering from knee surgery; there were new assistant coaches and coordinators; the kicking game was unsettled; and quarterback Eli Manning, on the threshold of his full third season, was in the midst of growing pains.

"It was a ridiculous downpour at 8:00 AM," Coughlin recalled, "and I am looking out the window saying, 'What are you doing?' When I got to the locker room, they were like, 'Let's go, Coach, we aren't going to stop the first practice with a little rain.'"

The unsettling signs had begun in February, when Barber publicly complained about Coughlin, who countered that the coaching staff had made Barber a far better player by curing his propensity for fumbles. In

Coughlin's first season, following a poor 2003 for Barber, the coaches addressed the problem. "He was very eager to learn this new technique and was an outstanding student," said Coughlin. "Everything he did throughout the off-season program was with the ball in the position that we call high and tight. To his credit, he mastered that particular technique to the point where in 2005 he had 411 touches and only one fumble. He's gone on to make the Pro Bowl three years in a row.... He had 200 and some yards rushing against Oakland in '05. He had 234 against Washington last year. I think he averaged 177 yards rushing in the last game of the year in '04, '05, and '06. And we did win the games. So while my regimen may be a grind, this is the first I've ever seen that or heard it from Tiki. We have a statement in our locker room that kind of sums that up: coaching is making players do what they don't want to do, so that they can become what they want to become."

Coughlin, the former head coach of the Jacksonville Jaguars, desperately wanted the Giants to become winners. His desire was so intense that he himself changed. Although he encouraged players to discuss things with him, Coughlin's single-mindedness and autocratic style had discouraged that type of communication.

Some players, like Manning, the younger brother of Peyton Manning, who had just won the Super Bowl with the Colts, immersed themselves in watching tape, and his accuracy improved while working with new quarterbacks coach Chris Palmer.

"I see improvement in terms of his ability to move his feet and to work well within the pocket, slide, to step up when he has to, to keep both hands on the ball, and then make an accurate throw," Coughlin said after one preseason game. "I think the indication is, if you remember a year ago, basically the same pattern, the crossing pattern that was not accurately thrown to Plaxico [Burress], basically the same thing last night to David Tyree, right on the money for what should have been a big play. He has worked hard on it, and certainly it has been reflected here in these games."

By mid-August, and with Strahan still not in camp and injuries piling up—Tyree fractured his wrist, and Burress, becoming one of Manning's favorite targets, was sidelined with back problems—reinforcements, and not necessarily household names, were brought in.

Asked by reporters about a lineman wearing No. 62, Coughlin said, "Sixty-two…. Do you have a program with you?"

After a reporter produced a program, one of them asked the coach, "How do you pronounce his name?"

"Tui, you mean?" Coughlin said. "Tui, yeah, don't ask me about the last name [Alailefaleula]. That supposedly is in writing somewhere, but I wouldn't even attempt to pronounce it, I'm sorry. I mean no disrespect, but I just can't get all those letters together. He is a large man."

Strahan was keeping in touch with the front office and several players, but the concern was mounting about his readiness to play—if he returned before the regular-season opener.

"You are talking about a guy who, provided he is in good health, provided he is mentally ready to go…the most impressive thing about Michael for me has always been that he comes out like a kid," said Coughlin. "He plays and practices like a young kid. And if he comes back in that frame of mind, and with that love of the game, then that's when he is going to be a big part of our team."

The players could appreciate Strahan's indecisiveness. Training camp, said center Shaun O'Hara, "is a strange thing. After every exit on 87 [the New York State Thruway], that is one last opportunity to turn around. Training camp does different things for different guys. It takes a lot of passion. You've got to really want to be here. Everybody contemplates it on the eve of training camp. We play it [training camp] for Sundays. That's why we do this."

Manning, meanwhile, a little scarred from not reaching the lofty expectations in the 2006 season, was maturing, And that prompted a prophetic comment from Coughlin. "I think that this year, although a difficult one, I think it's going to be a good one for him to learn from," the head coach said. "I think moving forward we feel that he still is the quarterback of the future of the New York Giants. We think he can win the Super Bowl."

Another young cog in the machinery was learning as well: the 6'4", fullback-like running back, Brandon Jacobs, the heir apparent to Barber. There was never any question about his ability to rumble downhill through opponents, to push the pile with his 240 pounds. But Jacobs was beginning to add another element to his game, one that would help Manning.

"He has also done a good job with his pass protection," Coughlin said after another preseason game. "Last night, they brought a Mike Sam X, they brought both linebackers in gaps, and he actually blocked both of them. He did a really good job of stacking them up."

But the mood of the team jumped significantly when a bearded leader finally showed up for practice.

"They all said I looked like Harrison Ford from *The Fugitive*," chirped Strahan. "The guys jumped on me from the beginning, they haven't let up, and that is what it is all about. It's about family, and these guys understood what I was going through and hopefully they play long enough where they can get to the point where they have that decision to make.... But it just boiled down to the fact that I looked and said, 'Hey, I want to play,' and I decided that I wanted to play. I wanted to get in here before I changed my mind."

When reporters asked if not having a Super Bowl ring was a factor, Strahan agreed. "I have Marshall Faulk and Warren Sapp and all those guys hitting me up all the time," he said. "I actually saw Marshall quite a bit this off-season. Those guys have the rings, so when I say to them, 'Hey Marshall, how is it to retire?' 'Great.' Yeah, you have a ring; it is a lot easier to leave that way. It is definitely something I want, hopefully something we can get here, and that is why I am here."

By September the pieces were in place.

But perhaps the most telling change was in taskmaster Coughlin himself. His "my way or the highway" grip loosened. For the first time in his diverse coaching career, he asked players to vote in secret ballots for permanent captains. The election results: Strahan and Antonio Pierce on defense; Manning and O'Hara on offense; and punter Jeff Feagles for special teams.

"I have certainly addressed issues that were brought to my attention," said Coughlin. "I have been at this for a long time and I believe that there is a certain way that these things are done. I think I can approach many things from a little bit different standpoint. To be honest with you, I thought over the course of the last eight games [last year] that in order to keep our team going...a lot of my approach changed. Those are things you would not know anything about. I have changed, but I also have things that I believe in, that I will hold true."

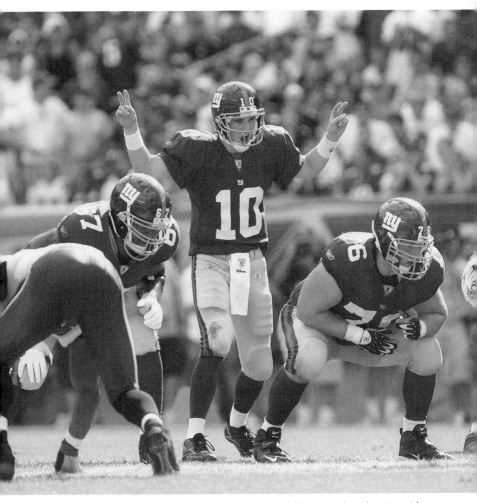

The maturation of quarterback Eli Manning would be critical to the Giants' hopes in 2007. Photo courtesy of Getty Images

Despite the cozier feelings, critics raised questions about the team's identity and their ability to win. "A lot of people don't know what to expect from this team," a writer said to Coughlin. "That's probably good," he answered. "Because what we would really like to do—and I've talked to our team about it—is let our playing do our talking for us and not spend so much time trying to explain who we are, where we are. Let's just play the game—talk is cheap—let's play the game."

The Giants opened the regular season in Dallas against the longtime rival Cowboys, and immediately, injuries cast a shadow on the club.

In a 45–35 loss, both Osi Umenyiora, a talented defensive end who was being mentored by Strahan, and Jacobs sustained knee injuries. Manning was 28-for-41 and threw four touchdowns, three to Burress, but sprained his shoulder. Backup Jared Lorenzen had to come in late in the game. A missed call angered Coughlin and brought out the "what-ifs."

"Late in the game, as poorly as we played on defense, we had an opportunity to win.... It is 38–35, third-and-7, they have an illegal procedure penalty, which is very obvious but not called, and they have a 51-yard touchdown. It would have been third-and-12, what happens there? You are going to have to punt the ball if you don't convert and then what happens? That having been said, we did not play very well on defense. We weren't as physical as we have been. We weren't as penetrating with our pressures. The quarterback only had a couple of times when he was hurried at all, we are disappointed in that.... We made a lot of big plays; we gave up a lot of big plays. We got outstanding performances out of a few people. Eli was very accurate. He had the ball on the money an awful lot of the time. He was under control in the game; made some outstanding throws even when he was pressured. There were a lot of young guys who got their first experience in the National Football League, and I think they will be better for it the next time we line up and play. I am disappointed. I am not discouraged."

Actually, discouragement reared its head in Week 2.

In the home opener against Brett Favre and the Packers, the Giants fell again, 35–13, and began 0–2 for the first time since 1996. "You can't let two games shake your confidence in a 16-game season," said new defensive coordinator Steve Spagnuolo. "Like anything that we all do, when you are in certain adverse situations, you rely on prior experiences. In 2000, and I think it was '03 or '02, we [in Philly] began 0–2. And we ended up in the NFC Championship Game. So it's not shaken me yet."

Manning admitted that he was not himself. He had missed Amani Toomer in the end zone and tight end Jeremy Shockey for another possible six. "That was kind of a roll right as I was trying throw back across my body," he said. "I just couldn't get enough on that one. It was a hard throw, and in that situation I floated a little too much and didn't get enough speed on it…. On Monday when I went in, the trainers said that usually this kind of injury takes a few weeks to get better. I knew from throwing after the injury, I had the kind of mindset that I could come back." But coming back wasn't enough. And the defense wasn't sharp. It was downright rusty.

On to Washington. In a game that, in retrospect, helped turn around the season, the Giants scored 14 points in the fourth quarter and made a gutsy goal-line stand in the final seconds, stuffing Ladell Betts to preserve a 24–17 lead for their first win. An 0–3 start would have been disastrous.

"We played well and won the fourth quarter, which is something I spoke about earlier in the week," said Coughlin. "As simple as it might be, that is what we wanted to try to do today—win the fourth quarter."

At 1–2, but with a dose of confidence, the Giants D was monstrous in Week 4.

The Eagles had scored 56 points the prior week, and everyone from fans to NFL pundits expected the defense would be tested. Instead, they blanked the Eagles for three quarters and wrecked their offensive line with a franchise-record-tying 12 sacks of Donovan McNabb, six by Umenyiora, mostly against Winston Justice, and one by Strahan that broke Lawrence Taylor's team record.

"Unbelievable game by the defense," guard David Diehl recalled. "Those guys definitely came to play. They got after the quarterback. The crowd got into it. It was a huge boost for our team. It was a huge boost for everything. Everybody kind of fed off of it. Congratulations to Michael Strahan. It is an unbelievable accomplishment to beat Lawrence Taylor for the all-time sacks. It doesn't get any better than that. Osi, if he isn't the defensive MVP of the week, I don't know what you need to get it. I talked about it all camp—being able to play up against him got me completely prepared for the season. Things didn't always go my way, but I knew the work I did against him would definitely pay off. It just shows the type of player that I knew he was."

In the fourth quarter, the defense was sitting on the bench, shaking their heads and laughing. "Everybody was just saying, 'It looked like a video game out there for you,'" Umenyiora recalled. "But Justice is a very good football player. Tonight was just one of those nights."

Even the oft-reserved Coughlin was animated on the sideline watching Umenyiora. "I am cheering," the red-cheeked coach said. "I am cheering like crazy: 'Get another one, get another one.'"

The Jets, who shared Giants Stadium with Big Blue, were up next. Rookie Aaron Ross, who won the Jim Thorpe Award as the nation's top defensive back while at the University of Texas in 2006, was benched to start the game for missing a meeting. Thanks to three interceptions and another big second half, the Giants gave Coughlin his 100th win and moved to 3–2.

"Three picks against [Chad] Pennington was big," said Strahan. "He doesn't make a lot of mistakes. They weren't just picks because our guys had to really jump on the ball. Our DBs played extremely well and made plays that got us through. We weren't looking too good in the first half team-wise, but I'm glad to see that we came out in the second half and shut them out." The Giants scored 28 points in those last 30 minutes en route to the 35–24 victory.

Ross said the temporary benching was a learning experience because he didn't feel shunned. "Coach didn't treat me like I was out of the game," the freshman from Texas said. "Every time the defense came to the sideline, I was in there with them getting the plays. I wouldn't say that I was out of the game, I just wasn't in the game out on the field."

Pennington said the Giants defense, especially the secondary, was outstanding. "They showed different looks on every snap," he said. "They did a good job of holding our running game down. A lot of times, people get on defensive backs saying the reason they aren't receivers is because they can't catch. These guys that we played today have really good hands. Anytime you have a defensive back that can catch the football and not just knock it down, that is a game-changing player and a game-changing play.... It's frustrating, and believe me, it makes you sick to your stomach. But that is the game of football."

At the Georgia Dome, the Giants routed the Falcons 31–10 for the 600th win in franchise history. Burress caught his eighth touchdown, Toomer became the Giants' all-time reception leader, Ross had his third pick in two weeks, and the defense dominated in the second half.

Even with the win, Umenyiora preached caution: "We have been 4–2 a couple of times over the last couple of years and we have seen how that ended, so I think everybody just has to maintain our focus. It seems like maybe the focus waned a little bit over the last couple of years, but this year we have seen what happens if we don't maintain our focus, and we can't allow that to happen."

No problem.

The following week in East Rutherford, the Giants led from the opening drive and never really looked back en route to a 33–15 pummeling of the 49ers. In the second half, the defense recorded six sacks (2.5 for Strahan, 1.5 for former Notre Dame captain Justin Tuck, one for Ross, and one for Umenyiora) and four turnovers, as the Giants raced to a 5–2 record for the fourth straight season.

Ups and Downs

A trip across the pond to England almost disrupted the Giants' momentum. But they eked out a 13–10 win at Wembley Stadium, serving the Dolphins their eighth loss and lifting themselves to 6–2.

Perhaps the most telling observations came from their former kicker, Dolphin Jay Feely. Asked if, when the Giants started 0–2, he thought they were dead and buried, Feely said, "I did. I think a lot of people felt that way just because of the way the season ended last year in New York. They weren't aggressive in free agency. They let a lot of players go and didn't really go out and try and replace those players. So the feeling was that they weren't going to be a great team this year. But I think people who knew about the team—like myself—knew how much talent there was there. But I think, without question, that credit has to go to Coach Coughlin. I have talked to a lot of the guys that obviously I am still friends with on the team. And they talked about the changes that he has made and whether it was because he felt like he didn't have anything to lose and wanted to try something different. But that is not easy for somebody to do; to change your ways. And I think that has really brought that team together. And I think another thing that probably did was Tiki Barber and the comments that he made against Eli and against Coach Coughlin. I think [that] really galvanized that team and the locker room to come together."

Feely, who was not re-signed and left as a free agent, said he foresaw what both Coughlin and the team would need for a revival. "I thought

Pick 'Em

What do you do for an encore if the first draft pick of your career as a general manager was John Elway? Keep swinging and hope to hit another homer.

Former Baltimore Colts and Cleveland Browns executive Ernie Accorsi, who chose quarterback Philip Rivers at No. 4 in order to maneuver a draft-day swap with San Diego for No. 1 pick Eli Manning, said he had no problem if he was going to be judged for picking Manning rather than Elway.

Before Manning ever came near reaching the Super Bowl in 2008, Accorsi said, "If that is the way it is, that it's the way it is." I have no problem with the percentage of that. I had eight teams in the playoffs and four championship games. In my mind I will look at the body of work. I won't be satisfied with it, don't get me wrong. But I'm just saying that there is a lot more besides him. But I have no problem being remembered for him [Manning]. I hope I live long enough to be able to enjoy it, that's all."

He would.

Not only did Manning win Super Bowl XLII, he was Super Bowl MVP. Asked if he felt he "gave away the moon and the solar system" to Eli Manning in his seven-year, $45 million contract, Accorsi gave this earthbound view: "I came in the league 35 years ago when the Baltimore Colts' payroll was $1 million. I rest my case. It's all the moon and solar system now."

as a locker room, and as leaders on our team, we talked too much and criticized Coach too much. And that our head coach needed unquestioned support, at least publicly, because otherwise you undermine his ability to lead," he said. "If you have a veteran question the head coach publicly, then those young guys are going to do that and they are not going to listen to him the way that they need to. I said that we needed that and then that Coach Coughlin could probably create a more friendly environment where players wanted to play for him more. I think that is exactly what has happened. Coach Coughlin took them out bowling and did little things like that to just try and relate to them on a level rather than just a football level."

Before the second meeting of the season against the Cowboys—this one in New Jersey—quarterbacks coach Chris Palmer was asked to compare Manning and Cowboys signal-caller Tony Romo, who had signed a six-year, $67.4 million contract. "They are very similar guys, good personality, want to win, want to compete, good guys to be around, and the guys relate to them," Palmer said. "Tony might be a little richer than him right now."

Manning, however, was gathering a wealth of knowledge. Palmer mentioned that Manning was calling audibles with more authority, even in the running game. "A tremendous amount of study, tremendous feel," he said. "When I grade the film, there is more than once that I would say on his grade sheet, 'outstanding check.'... There is instinct, there is film study—you have to spend a lot of time studying other teams, and he does that. When you as a coach say, 'Hey, did you see this game?' 'Yeah, I saw it,' 'Did you see this play?' 'Yeah, I saw that play, what did you think it was?' That is a guy that takes his profession very, very seriously."

The Dallas game was nationally televised, and naturally the hype was spreading. The Giants wanted to convince the doubters. "I think my parents are waiting to see how good we really are," said Manning. "Even though you win six games in a row, it's like, 'Oh, you won six games, but look who they won them against,' it is always that way. We could have beat the Patriots, and still it would be, 'Well, they beat one good team, but the other guys....' You can never please everybody, but for us, we realized that at some point you go from being lucky to good. You don't win six games from being lucky, especially in this league."

Well, win number seven would have to wait.

The Cowboys toppled the Giants for the second time in the season, 31–20, and Cowboys receiver Patrick Crayton discussed the buildup. "They've been talking all week," he said. "I think when you are kind of scared of another team like that, I think you kind of have to talk yourself up to really give yourself a chance. It started with Brandon Jacobs and it kind of trickled a little bit to some other players. I don't know why he was talking. He had a good rushing game, but in the end they lost."

At Ford Field in Detroit, the Giants improved to 7–3, thanks in large part to Lawrence Tynes' three field goals in a 16–10 game, in what turned out to be perhaps the most forgettable win of the season. The offense struggled, and linebacker Mathias Kiwanuka broke his left leg, finishing him for the campaign.

The following week, the Giants were drubbed by the Vikings 41–17. Manning was intercepted four times—with three returned for touchdowns.

Coughlin almost pulled Manning, who was hit or on the ground more than he had been all year. "I thought about it at one point, it was the fourth quarter, but I didn't see the purpose in that, either," he said. "I just don't like that feeling. I wasn't going to do that, I wasn't going to do that to him and I wasn't going to do that to me, and us."

Said Rich Seubert, whose mates on the offensive line were awful: "Obviously, things didn't go the way we wanted them to. We just couldn't get it turned around. This is on all of us. It is probably the worst game I have been a part of as a New York Giant. I'm embarrassed, and I'm sure a lot of other guys are here, too. We have to find a way to turn it around. We are still 7–4. We have five big games left. And we could still be there."

Sensing that the slide could continue against the always-tough Bears, Coughlin called out his troops. "I told the team that this is the real test right now, that it is not about a man and the fact that he gets knocked down, it is what he does after he gets back up," Coughlin said at the time. "It is the first game of a five-game season for us. I think they will respond well, but I think this, too: we have to perform at a much higher level. There is a lot of pride involved and there is a lot of looking at that tape and asking themselves, 'Why did that happen? How did I do that? Why didn't I do that?' And I think from the standpoint of the quality of our play again and being as good as we can possibly be, that stuff has got to happen pretty darn fast."

Down 16–7 in the fourth quarter at Soldier Field in Chicago, Manning completed a 6-yard scoring pass to Toomer, and backup running back Reuben Droughns plunged over from the two-yard line. Giants 22, Bears 16. Coughlin called it divine intervention.

"By the grace of God, we are 8–4. It looked bleak, but we kept playing," he said. "Our defense kept getting the ball back. We got into the situation where we needed two scores. We got into the no-huddle, and things started to settle down."

Punter Jeff Feagles kept the ball away from kick-return dynamo Devin Hester. And Coughlin won a challenge on the Toomer touchdown catch. "Amani thought he caught the ball," the coach declared. "Thank goodness we had our challenge to use. There was no way we were not going to use it."

Coughlin's Code

Tom Coughlin is never shy about his code—or the fact that he admires coaches with the same philosophy. "What I have always been all about is a solid work ethic. What I saw when I traveled reinforced that to the greatest extent. Dick Vermeil, for example. I was there early in camp, and they worked in pads one morning for two and a half hours, and afternoon practice was the same way. When I went to visit Bill [Parcells] in San Antonio, they put the pads on and went to work. They practiced twice a day. They worked hard. They had great focus. Dom Capers was the same exact way. Jim Haslett over in New Orleans—those were the four camps that I went to and I saw what I believed in: football players taking pride in being football players and going about the business of becoming a football team. Football is a contact sport. It is a physical sport. We are all in the business of the salary cap and we all understand the ramifications, but as I heard Parcells quote one day: 'You can't protect the players, you have to get them ready to play.'"

Asked what went thorough his mind when rookie quarterback Eli Manning took a vicious hit in one of his first games, Coughlin simply said: "Welcome to the NFL, son."

In a revealing postgame discourse, Coughlin also buried some myths about halftime adjustments. "Many people have misconceptions about what goes on in those 12 minutes," he said. "You and your coaches huddle, put together your ideas, look at what you had for a plan, and you decide if you're going to alter it or stay with it. In the fourth quarter, we really had to pass. We went back to some of our play-action stuff we had prepared. It was all prepared for our last game that we had ready to go. We just found time to use it."

Strahan praised Manning's rebound from the criticism during the week following the loss. "When you think about a Brett Favre, the one thing that they always say about [him] is: 'He's a gunslinger. He'll throw a pick and keep slinging.' As a player who would play with him, you'd love that. You want a quarterback who's fearless, who's not afraid to make a mistake. All of us make mistakes. And for Eli to stand up, come back and do those things, hopefully that builds some confidence in him because really, that's all his game is."

The comeback against the Bears carried over into the rematch with the Eagles, which turned out to be a nail-biter at The Linc in Philadelphia. The Giants emerged with a hard-fought 16–13 win when

David Akers bounced a 57-yard field goal try off the right upright with one second left in regulation.

Burress, who by now had forged some impressive chemistry with Manning, said: "I guess he gets that feeling like, 'Okay, 17 is ready to go today.' We get in a rhythm, he notices it, the coaches notice it, and we just kept going to it, making big plays. When [Eli] goes out and plays like he did today, our offense can do whatever it wants. I have been saying for a long time, that when he plays well, our offense plays well, and we can get better and better. Down the road, we are going to need to make plays in the intermediate passing game, because the weather is not going to be so good. We will need to catch some short balls and turn them into big plays."

Asked about the 9–4 team's personality, fans heard vintage Strahan. "The personality? I don't know but I know it's one that's going to give me a heart attack if we keep winning like this," he said. "I think the personality of this team is that guys are going to play for four quarters. We're not going to quit, we're always going to fight. We believe we have a chance to win, no matter if it's on the road or home. Whatever the circumstances, we're going to play for four quarters and play for each other. I think that's it. Have accountability to each other."

The difference between the 2006 and 2007 Giants, Toomer said, was simple: "Attitude. Attitude. We had a lot of adversity early in the season. We didn't know if 92 [Strahan] was going to be here. We didn't have Tiki. There was concern about our secondary not being able to fit. On top of all that, guys continued to believe in one another. There's been no real finger-pointing, no bickering and complaining. When you don't

Lightening Eli's Wallet

When first-round draft pick Eli Manning signed a seven-year deal worth about $45 million with the Giants before showing up at training camp, Michael Strahan knew his wallet might be a little thicker as well. No, he wasn't planning to renegotiate his contract; he just wasn't footing the bill for two anymore. "I haven't had a chance to congratulate him," said Strahan. "I hung out with Eli a lot in the off-season and now I don't feel bad about making him pay. I've been picking up the tab because he hadn't signed yet, and I didn't want him to have to ask [brother] Peyton for money, now he can pay [for] himself."

have that, guys just come in and have fun day in and day out, and whatever happens on the football field, we take it as men."

The sellout crowd for the Sunday night game against the Washington Redskins at Giants Stadium left disappointed. The offense never found much traction, and Jeremy Shockey broke his left fibula in the third quarter, ending his season. The only touchdown in the 22–10 loss came from Shockey's sub, Kevin Boss, who caught a 19-yard pass from Manning and almost lost a memento of his first NFL score. "I guess I tossed it to the official and I came over to the sideline," Boss recalled. "And everyone was saying, 'Where is the football?' and I was like, 'Oh, shoot, I forgot,' but I think [Joe] Skiba ran it down and got it."

The Giants didn't have their prize yet, either. At 9–5, they were without a playoff berth in the NFC East.

The weather in Buffalo, where the Giants brought their 6–1 road record and a chance to clinch a postseason invite, was typical for that Canadian border city: snowy, windy, rainy. Not the type of day for Manning again. But here's where the balance of a playoff-bound team showed. The running game excelled in the elements. Jacobs (143 yards rushing, two TDs) and Ahmad Bradshaw (151 yards and one TD), steamrolled the Bills in a 38–21 victory. At 10–5, the wild-card was theirs.

Now the strategic question was: do you rest some key players against the 15–0 Patriots or go punch-for-punch? "New England is New England," said Strahan, "and we are going to give them everything we got, whether it's our starters or our backups or a half. Whatever Coach decides to do, that's what is going to happen. We're not going out there to lay down for them, and they aren't going to lay down for us."

Anyone who really thought Coughlin, the receivers coach in New York under Bill Parcells, the former Boston College head coach and the man who guided the Jaguars to two AFC Championship Games, would ease up on the throttle, was, well, just loony.

"We're never going to just rest," he said. "Even if [New England] wasn't 15–0, we're going to go in there and try to win the football game. You never want to lose the edge that you have mentally. You can't relax a little bit going into the playoffs. All of our starters are expected to play, and we're going to attack it."

The anticipation of a perfect regular season was so overwhelming that CBS, NBC, and the NFL Network simulcast the game—the first time in history that one NFL game was carried on three networks.

Although the Giants stunned fans by leading 28–16 in the third quarter, the Tom Brady–to–Randy Moss combination pulled the Patriots through to a 38–35 win. But the Giants emerged with an infusion of confidence that would be vital over the next weeks.

"That is the best team in the league, probably hands down, in the regular season," said linebacker Antonio Pierce. "I thought we played toe-to-toe with those guys. But you have to play four quarters. I think we have to look at all of the positives and fix the negatives. I think we played exceptional all across the board. We only turned the ball over once [a Manning interception to go along with his four TDs] and gave up one big play on defense. You have to play damn near perfect against them—you have to play perfect."

Said Tuck, the defensive lineman who would play a huge role in the Giants' future, "This is a pretty good momentum builder.... We are still disappointed because you don't want to lose. But I think it gives us the gauge that we wanted. We definitely wanted to win it, but they are 16–0 for a reason."

Little did Tuck, or anyone, realize that there would be a rematch with the undefeated Patriots—in the biggest game of all.

On to the Playoffs

The pirate ship and the 65,621 fans at Raymond James Stadium were rocking in anticipation of the wild-card game in Tampa Bay. After all, Manning had not won a playoff game, and Coughlin hadn't won one with the Giants.

"This team really likes the road," Pierce told anyone who would listen. "I look forward to it because of the extra incentive when you're getting booed by the whole stadium because they dislike you. You're hearing reports that you're not going to win. To me, this is the best team in the NFL with their backs against the wall and when everybody throws everything at them. We don't need any pats on the butt at all."

Manning did not start well: the team had −2 yards of offense in the first quarter, and the Bucs led 7–0. But Manning adjusted, and the Giants took a 14–7 cushion into halftime. Corey Webster, who would intercept a Jeff Garcia pass in the end zone later in the quarter, recovered a fumble on the second-half kickoff, and Tynes converted for a 17–7 lead. Manning, who was 20-of-27 for 185 yards, connected with Toomer for the 24–14 final.

"We have been in the playoffs the last three seasons, and I haven't played particularly well in the two games before, and just to come in here and play well, give our team a chance to win the game, and make some big plays, that was quite a situation to be in," Manning said. "I think they [his teammates] still believe in me. They have faith that I can make plays and we can win. We have been doing it all season, we've won all sorts of different types of games. So I think we just have to keep finding ways to win."

Before the next game against the Cowboys—the third of the season between the two franchises—Coughlin was asked about how close the success of the offense was tied to Manning. "I would say hip-to-hip. Tied at the wherever," he responded.

The Las Vegas oddsmakers were hip to that as well, making the Giants 7½-point underdogs, which prompted this taste of sarcasm from Pierce. "Hopefully we will get a little closer than that," he said. "To be honest, they have more pressure on them than we do. We are just the 10–6 Giants against the No. 1–seed Cowboys, who are going to win the Super Bowl."

The Cowboys were rested, having come off a bye week, yet still made headlines, when Romo, his Page Six girlfriend, and some players went on a vacation by the sea.

Said Strahan: "You guys love to say, 'Oh, he is coming off the beach, and he is dating Jessica Simpson.' Please. Heck, if Jessica Simpson wanted to date me, I may give her a shot. I can't blame the guy. It's your bye week, you can do whatever you want to do. If he wanted to sit in Dallas, they would have found some fault in that because he would have been with her. So for them to go to Cabo, or wherever they went, good for them. They deserve that time off. I think anybody who thinks that because he took a few days with his girlfriend that he is going to come back and not play well or he is not going to be prepared…if anything, it probably stokes his fire to play even better."

As for his team, Strahan rejected the notion that the Giants would be tight: "The thing that surprised me about Coach Coughlin is he came up to me last week and said, 'I just want the guys to remember to have fun.' Now, that is not a word you associate with Coughlin: *fun*. They don't go together, but in this case, it does. That showed me that he understands that we have been winning and we have been playing well because guys have been loose, because guys are enjoying being around."

They certainly enjoyed the 21–17 result, which advanced them to the NFC Championship Game for the first time since 2000.

"It's unbelievable," said Toomer, who caught two Manning throws for touchdowns. "To get an opportunity to come in here and play against a team that has already beaten us twice this season was great. When I was walking off the field the last time, I was thinking to myself that I wish we had an opportunity to play them again. We got that chance and beat them when it counted."

It wasn't a cakewalk. Defense reigned in the second half, which began tied at 14. In fact, the Giants had a chance to run out the clock with two minutes to play, but went three-and-out.

"It was such a disappointment on our part, because the defense was doing a great job the whole time," said guard Chris Snee. "Really, if we get a first down, it would have iced the game. You can't give Romo too many chances. For the most part, I had my head buried in my hands and I just waited for the reaction of the sidelines."

With 90 seconds left in the game, Romo drove the Cowboys downfield, but R.W. McQuarters picked off a pass in the end zone with nine seconds left. Manning took a knee and thought about facing the 14–3 Packers with a chance to go to the Super Bowl.

"We didn't make any mistakes on offense, not many, if any, penalties, and their defense did a great job at the end," said Manning. "So did ours; holding their offense to 17 points hasn't been done many times this season. Amani Toomer catching that ball on the first series and taking it to the house was big. Then getting the ball back after their offense kept it for 10 minutes in the second quarter with 47 seconds left and going down the field and scoring was big as well."

At Lambeau Field, the temperature was appropriate for January 20: with the windchill factor, it was −23.

"The coldest game I've played," said kicker Lawrence Tynes. "It's [kicking the ball] like kicking cardboard." Nonetheless, Tynes hit two field goals for an early 6–0 lead over the Packers. But Brett Favre found Donald Driver busting past a chuck by Corey Webster for a 90-yard catch-and-run, and Green Bay led 10–6 at the half. The Giants would have to stage yet another revival, this time on the legendary frozen tundra.

"Me and Amani and Plaxico came out about two hours before the game to do our warmup, and we only got through about a quarter of it," Manning recalled. "We said, 'Hey, we've got to go in.' My left hand was numb, my receivers, they didn't have any hand warmers, they were done. I said, 'Hey, I can throw. Let's take it in. We're good.' But on the sideline they had the heaters. I stood by that the whole game. I never took my helmet off. I just stood by the heater, stayed warm. I had big gloves around my hand. I kept my hand warm, that was the main thing."

It worked. Remember how Burress had said that late in the season, shorter throws would be critical? Burress caught 11 of Manning's 21 completions for 151 of the quarterback's 251 yards. "There was a lot of single high man-to-man coverage, and we had some big plays," said Manning. "We hit a couple, we call it fade stops, where he goes outside, and you just make a read. If he gets on top, you throw the read, and if not, you throw it up high and let him use his body. He's a hard guy to stop when you have that play on."

At 20–20 in the fourth quarter, though, it came down to kicking. Tynes missed a 43-yarder with less than seven minutes to play, and with four seconds to play, bent a 36-yarder on a bad snap. The Packers won the toss, and Favre tried to find Driver on an out pattern. But Webster atoned for his earlier miscue, cutting to the ball and returning it to the 34. Three plays later, Tynes lined up for a 47-yarder.

"I just ran on the field," Tynes said. "I knew it was going to be close to 50, but I knew I could get it there. He [Coughlin] had to make a decision when I was out there lining up to kick it. I kind of made the decision for him. I wasn't going to let him say, "Go kick." He would have had to pull me off the field."

On the sideline, Manning thought, "He can make this one. There's no reason why. We've got another shot, we've got another opportunity. He's made big field goals for us before, and it just seems like we just like to put ourselves in those situations. We like to make it tough on ourselves. We can't make the short one and win at home, but we can win on the road, make the 47-yard field goal in overtime just to make it exciting."

Tynes didn't miss. "I knew if everything worked out that I could make the kick," he remembered. "The last one was good snap, good hold. A little bit further, but there was a little bit of wind helping us that way."

Improbably, the Giants had won 10 straight games on the road, all three playoff road games, and were headed to the Super Bowl in a much warmer climate: Glendale, Arizona.

Tynes, asked how he would have reacted had he not gotten that third opportunity, was resolute. "I'm not thinking about that. I made the game-winning kick that got us in the Super Bowl," he said. "Maybe one day I'll say, 'Holy cow, what if I would have missed it?'"

Manning and other players pointed to the Patriots' regular-season game as the beginning of their extraordinary finishing kick. "We played well, kind of got us going a little bit, got us feeling good and have been on a roll since and playing good football," he said. "We've been a streaky team. We've gone on streaks before. It seems like we lost the first two and then you win six in a row. We'd kind of lose a little bit in and out, and now we've found it again, so hopefully we can keep it going."

Watching from the sideline as the ball flew in the darkness over the cross bar, Coughlin was overcome with emotion and memories. "I'm happy for so many other people that I don't even...it hasn't struck me yet, really," he said. "I'm happy for Mrs. Mara, Mrs. Tisch [the widows of the late owners]. I was asked the other day, do I ever think about Mr. Mara and Mr. Tisch. Yeah, we do. I'm happy for them, as well. I'm happy for my family, to be honest with you, for my wife and for my kids and for all those that hung in there and battled away. And I'm happy for our players, because you start out 0–2, and you start right back on the tread-mill again, and you start with the negatives, and you have to fight your way back. And of course the way we went into Washington and were able to win, and the fact now that we've won 10 straight games on the road, which is a record, franchise record, NFL record, you name it. And we are the NFC champions, it's a wonderful tribute to these guys. Because as two or three of them mentioned to me when we were in the locker room, they believed, we believed. Not many others did, but we did, and that's the reason we're here."

A Super Bowl for the Ages

The Patriots and their fans envisioned the Super Bowl as a coronation. The confident, undefeated club, led by coach Bill Belichick, tried to trademark the numerals 19–0. On the field at the University of Phoenix Stadium, a few borderline-arrogant New England players invited the Giants to their victory celebration.

The Giants—12-point underdogs—had a three-pronged focus: Hit Tom Brady. Stop the run. Win the fourth quarter.

They did all three.

The MVP quarterback was knocked down 23 times and sacked five; the Patriots managed just 45 yards on the ground; and Plaxico Burress—double-covered much of the game and with just one catch—caught the game-winner with 39 seconds left for a 17–14 Giants win, one of the greatest Super Bowl upsets in history. "We shocked the world," Strahan said amid a rain of red-and-blue confetti. "We shocked ourselves."

The opening drive set the tone. Mixing runs and short passes, the Giants ran 16 plays and held the ball for 9:59, a Super Bowl record, capped by Tynes' 32-yard field goal. Laurence Maroney scored from the 1 on the first play of the second quarter, giving the Patriots a 7–3 edge.

But the defense stiffened, and Tuck's second sack, in the final seconds of the half, forced a Brady fumble that was pounced on by Umenyiora. The most prolific offense in NFL history, triggered by Brady's 50 touchdowns, had gained just 81 yards.

The teams banged helmet-to-helmet in a scoreless third quarter, but on the opening drive of the fourth, Manning produced an 80-yard drive, climaxing with David Tyree's five-yard grab on a slant for a touchdown.

But 10–7 wouldn't be enough. Brady, finally getting some protection, engineered an eight-pass, 80-yard drive, and with 2:45 to play,

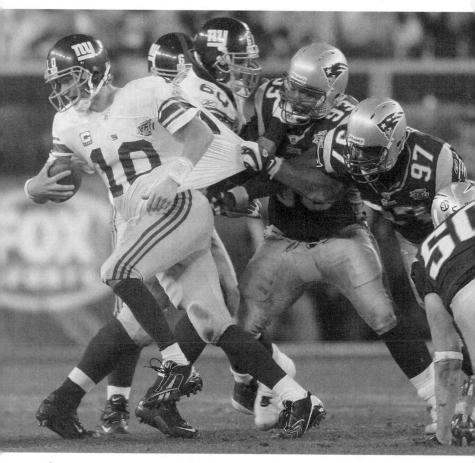

Eli Manning miraculously escapes the grasp of Patriots lineman Richard Seymour to begin one of the greatest plays in Super Bowl history. Photo courtesy of Getty Images

found Randy Moss from six yards out after cornerback Corey Webster slipped for a 14–10 lead.

Then, one of the epic drives in Giants history, with numerous crucial plays, began on the Giants' 17. On fourth-and-1 at the 37, Brandon Jacobs slammed ahead for two yards. Manning scrambled for five and then threw a deep pass that fortunately bounced off the hands of cornerback Asante Samuel.

Given new life, Manning and Tyree made a play for the ages, one that will live on YouTube, highlight reels, and in the minds of fans forever. It was third-and-5 on the 44. From the shotgun, Manning stepped up to avoid an outside charge from Adalius Thomas. Richard Seymour and Jarvis Green pushed up the middle and both grabbed Manning's jersey, but somehow he spun away, raced back a few yards, and saw Tyree about 30 yards downfield. With Rodney Harrison on him, Tyree leapt and snagged Manning's desperate floater at the 24. He bent backward from Harrison's tackle, but Tyree miraculously pinned the ball to his helmet with his right hand.

"There were two or three guys who had him [Manning], and he breaks free and throws up a Hail Mary that the guy comes down with," said Harrison.

Manning never saw the catch except on the highlights. "People were asking me how I got out of that jam I was in, and I really don't know," he said. "They were pulling me down. I felt them holding me, but I never felt anybody pull me to the ground. I stayed alive and I saw David in the middle of the field. I gave him a shot to make the catch, and...unbelievable catch. For him to catch that ball—kind of hold it against his helmet—I think he pulled back and guys [were] swiping at the ball. It's just a great individual effort."

Said Coughlin: "That play will go down as one of the biggest ever."

But the Giants needed seven points, not three. On third down, after a Thomas sack and an incompletion, Manning connected with Steve Smith, who stepped out of bounds at the 13.

Burress, doubled-teamed all day and limited to one catch, lined up wide left and somehow had just one defender, Ellis Hobbs, on him. The Patriots had decided on a first-down, seven-man blitz, leaving just four players to defend the pass. Here was where the countless hours of study and film paid dividends for Manning. He recognized the coverage; Burress ran a fake slant-and-go, Hobbs bought it inside, and Manning lofted a fade into the end zone that Burress cradled with 35 seconds left. "That's a position you want to be in," said Manning, "You can't write a better script. There were so many big plays on that drive."

Down 17–14, the Patriots had one final opportunity. But rookie long snapper Jay Alford, an Orange, New Jersey, native, leveled Brady on an inside rush for a 10-yard loss on second down with 19 seconds left.

Manning eventually took a knee, and the Giants became the first NFC wild-card team to win a Super Bowl.

"The right moment, the right time, every team is beatable," said Coughlin. It was the Giants' third Super Bowl win, but for Wellington Mara's son, John, the sweetest. "It's the greatest victory in the history of this franchise, without question," he said.

And with a remarkable season behind them, the stories and the reflections came to the surface. "We had a lot of big plays at the end," said Manning. "Amani Toomer had a big third-down catch. We had a fourth-and-1 conversion. Steve Smith on third-and-10. You could see the end zone, we were getting close and we still had a lot of work. He had a great catch on the sideline to be able to get up the field and get the first down, and get out of bounds to stop the clock. The offensive line was doing their job protecting, and everybody had their part and their role. [New England] had been playing zone, keeping two safeties back and just playing a little conservative through that whole drive. Finally, I knew they'd come after us. They came out with a blitz and had one-on-one with Plaxico Burress. That's a match-up we're going to take every time. He ran a great route, got wide open, and made a great catch."

Manning dished out the kudos like a seasoned veteran, not a 27-year-old. "We never lost our belief that we could make a big run," he said. "At the end of the season, we were playing our best football. That's what you want to be doing. At the end of the season, you want to be at your best. We got hot at the right time going into the playoffs. We played, really, five great games at the end of the season, the first being against the Patriots the last game, and then the four after.... If I could give [the Super Bowl MVP trophy] to the whole team, I would. To win a championship, everybody has to do their part. Our entire defense and that defensive front, the way that they got after Tom Brady and the way that they were able to get pressure on him, no one has been able to do that all year. The Giants' defensive staff and the way those guys played, they all deserve it. David Tyree, Plaxico, Amani Toomer, and Steve Smith, we had so many guys with big plays during the game, and that's what it takes. You never know who is going to have that opportunity to make a play. When the guys' numbers were called, they made every play that was out there to be made."

Watching from the stands, older brother Peyton Manning, to whom Eli will forever be compared, was jubilant. "[Peyton] came into the locker room after the game and he was just fired up and said that the play to [David] Tyree will go down as one of the great plays in NFL history," Eli said. "I saw highlights of him jumping up when we got the touchdown throw to Plaxico, and he was excited."

To succeed, the younger Manning had accepted the challenges, both of becoming a championship quarterback and guiding the evolution of a championship team. "I think it's just a great tribute to this Giants team, the organization, and coaches for continuing to have faith in ourselves and in the team," said Manning, the New Orleans native who was selected first overall in the 2004 draft by the Chargers, but had previously stated that he did not want to play for San Diego. Manning was

David Tyree clutches a crucial third-down pass to his helmet in the Giants' upset of the Patriots in Super Bowl XLII. Photo courtesy of Getty Images

sent to the Giants for Philip Rivers, the fourth overall pick, a third-round selection, and the Giants' first- and fifth-round picks in 2005.

The swap engineered by Accorsi had paid the ultimate dividend.

"I never doubted myself," Manning said. "I never lost confidence. As a quarterback, I think that's the most important thing, that you never lose confidence in yourself. You're going to go through a lot. When you're not playing well and when you're losing games, they're going to look into everything you do and dissect it—my demeanor or how I am on the sidelines, and my personality. But I'm very comfortable in my own skin. I am the way I am and I wasn't going to change. I love being in New York. I knew I was in the right place. It just takes time."

From his perch as a coach, Coughlin saw the progression in Manning, from draft pick to the pinnacle. "The thing that always struck me about the New York Giants when I was an assistant coach was the way in which George Young and Bill Parcells approached the peaks and valleys," he said. "They didn't want any of those. That's one of the great characteristics that Eli has. He knows how to handle praise and knows what comes with criticism, as well. That has served him very, very well. He is as competitive as any guy that I've ever been around. He was sitting in my office in his rookie year after the Baltimore and Washington experience—where he was blitzed pretty much every down. He was frustrated and hadn't played well. He kind of lost his poise a couple times and just sat there in my office [saying], 'Coach, I want to be good. I want to be the quarterback of the New York Giants. I want to lead the New York Giants to victory.' You saw some of that emotion pouring out of him. He's got it deep inside. He masks it very, very well. His development has been very, very steady. You all know, he has great, great games. The Philadelphia game at the beginning of the season a year ago, the unbelievable comeback and unbelievable finish to that game. Quite frankly, Eli plays very, very well in that circumstance, the no-huddle, the two-minute drill. There have been some games that were not what Eli would have wanted. He comes right back and applies himself again. As he went into the playoffs, it's very important to remember that he focused and concentrated, and literally eliminated the turnovers. He also did that in all kinds of extremes. He played in very cold weather in Green Bay and threw the ball with great accuracy.

He played in Tampa in 78 degrees. He was able to play his game despite what else was going on around him. That was a great lesson for his teammates and for the world to see."

On the day after the most satisfying win of his coaching career, a long journey from that rainy morning in Albany and thousands of practices in colleges and the pros, Coughlin delivered an eloquent summary, from Xs and Os to the human side of sports.

"The thing that happened in the playoffs that hadn't happen over the course of the year," he said, "was that we began to gain some advantages with turnovers. We stopped turning the ball over offensively and on special teams, and we played really good defensive football and were able to [force] turnovers and give ourselves some opportunities to have the ball a few more times than we had been having it. The real distinguishing factor was that we just kept getting better and our confidence grew. Our players actually felt that they could win under any circumstance. Each game that we approached, they believed it. We used the phrase, 'Believe it. Feel it.' And they did. We practiced that way. We prepared that way. We knew going into all of these games that the margin of victory was very small. We would have to play at a championship level in order to win. We were able to do that."

Facing the Patriots in Week 17, he asserted again, was a major asset. "I really felt, and our players did too," said Coughlin, "that if you're going to go into something that is hard, why not prepare with something that's very hard? Our players wanted to play against the Patriots and have a chance to win. We believed that we had a great chance to win in that game. The way we approached it was that we would play as hard as we could, do all that we possibly could to win the game. As I told the players, there would be nothing but positives out of the game. As it turns out, it was a great bridge for us from the regular season and into the playoffs because the caliber of our play just continued to escalate."

On the day before the Super Bowl, Coughlin had told the players "a little bit of my personal experience, having been an assistant coach on a Super Bowl champion. I wanted that for each one of them, because describing it is very difficult. The sensation and the feel from a professional standpoint—I'm not talking about family—the professional standpoint, when you win and realize that you are the world champion,

Wide receiver Plaxico Burress hauls in the game-winning touchdown pass to complete one of the greatest upsets in Super Bowl history. Photo courtesy of Getty Images

it's a tremendous, tremendous feeling. It's one that permeates everything that you do. When Eli began talking about family after the game is another thing that I told the players about, is the way that your family embraces being a world champion as well. That really, to me, gave me great satisfaction. Seeing my wife and my children and their children and husbands, wives, et cetera, and their reaction.... I opened the door to my room this morning [Monday], and my son Tim was in the hallway dressed in a jogging suit. I said, 'What are you doing? What are you doing up?' He said, 'I didn't sleep. I watched the game twice.' He has two little [kids] and he's up all night watching a couple times over.

"I told the players, it's good to dream. It's good to dream and visualize and see yourself in those circumstances and situations. It's funny, because when I was right out of college as a Division III coach going from club football to varsity football, my college teammate, Larry Csonka, was playing very, very well in the pro game. Actually, that was the '72 season, the undefeated season [for Miami]. In watching the way in which he impacted the game, you dream. You always dream."

chapter 2

Coming of Age: Simms to Bavaro

One was a brash, preppy kid who was born in his grandfather's stately antebellum home—now on the National Register of Historic Places—nestled amid 15 acres of rolling, bluegrass hills in Springfield, Kentucky.

The other was a quiet, blue-collar youngster born in Winthrop, Massachusetts, a Boston harbor town whose diverse natives include poet Sylvia Plath and guitarist Steven Van Zandt of the E Street Band.

How these two athletes, quarterback Phil Simms and tight end Mark Bavaro, discovered championship chemistry on the pro football stages of America in the mid-1980s while playing for the New York Giants—particularly in the magical 1986 season, which ended in the franchise's first Super Bowl trophy—is a tale worth revisiting.

Allegiances like these are strong and refuse to fade. Long after he had become a successful broadcaster with CBS, Simms was asked whom he would look for downfield if he had to complete a pass to win a Super Bowl now.

"It's hard to go away from an old teammate," he said. "I'd go to Mark Bavaro. We had a rule with the Giants: when he was covered, throw it to him anyway."

Phillip Martin Simms, who was called "Whitey" by his classmates, didn't throw the ball much in high school or college. Henderson Wilson was his coach at Southern High School in Louisville, where the Simms family had moved, "and I can't tell you how old-school he was,"

Simms once recalled. "He'd be like, 'Men, we're not gonna throw the ball at all today, we're just gonna run, run, run,' and I'd think, 'Great.'"

That wasn't what the confident, strong-armed quarterback of the Southern High Trojans wanted to hear. "You didn't talk to the coach in those days, and I certainly didn't," Simms remembered. "I was scared to death of him. I remember the one time I did, we were near the end of a game we needed to make the playoffs, and it was fourth-and-5. On the sideline he asked me, 'Well, what do you want to do?' and I came up with a play and completed a pass, and we won. But that was the only conversation we ever had."

After graduating in 1974, Simms attended Morehead State University, which—surprise!—also featured a ball-control offense. Perhaps his Eagles receivers were rusty from the inactivity—and perhaps because he wasn't always a beacon of accuracy—Simms completed just 48.9 percent of his passes, with 32 touchdowns and 45 interceptions over four years. The Eagles were 2–6–1 in his senior year, but Simms held the school record in yardage with 5,545 and had been named player of the year in the Ohio Valley Conference in 1977.

Coaches from about 10 NFL teams made the trek to Louisville, but the most intriguing, according to Simms, was the pre-draft visit from Bill Walsh, who had just taken the reins of the San Francisco 49ers, and his assistant, Sam Wyche.

At the start of the workout, Simms started rearing back and firing passes as usual, and Walsh stopped him, asking him to throw softer, to concentrate on pace, on spirals that receivers could catch. "Nobody ever taught me that," he recalled. "I was told to drop back and throw hard." Walsh told him to ease into the drop-back, to step lightly, to find a rhythm. The lesson in technique was startling. "I thought, *The guy's been here about 15 minutes, and I feel like a machine*," Simms said.

During a later visit, Simms was even more impressed. Walsh told him that the 49ers were planning on selecting him in the third round. The Giants, however, beat Walsh to the draw; they had a first-round selection, San Francisco didn't.

In 1978 the Giants had hired George Young, a former personnel director in Miami and assistant coach in Baltimore, as general manager. Young also liked what he saw in Simms. "Every once in a while you get

Phil Simms was an unknown quarterback at Morehead State before leading the Giants to victory in Super Bowl XXI. Photo courtesy of Getty Images

Education of a Rookie

Sometimes coaches use newspapers—not films—to teach young players a thing or two. Giants defensive coordinator Tim Lewis had a clipping to show Gibril Wilson.

"Joey Thomas, a defensive back…made a comment to a person in Green Bay," said Lewis. "I guess one of the press people wrote something about how he feels now as opposed to last year, and he said: 'I thought I knew what I was doing but I had no earthly idea.' He said, 'I'm much more comfortable now that I've gone through it.' For guys that are rookies coming into the NFL and they think they know what they are doing and they think they know what they are getting into, trust me, you have no idea what you are getting ready to go through. It is like going from your freshman year to your sophomore year in college. You think you know because you were really good in high school, but you have no clue. I'm going to show [Wilson] that article. Last year, he just ran around like a chicken with his head cut off and made some plays and had some fun. This year he's going to have to know what to do. He's not going to be a surprise to anyone anymore."

a chance to get a guy with a great arm and great potential and you'd darn right better take it," Young said at the time.

On draft day in New York, Simms, who acknowledged that "most people haven't heard of me," was selected No. 7 overall, surprising the Giants fans in attendance, who greeted Commissioner Pete Rozelle's announcement with boos. Because the television cameras missed Rozelle's initial announcement, he was asked to reprise it. The disgruntled fans booed again.

Walsh and the 49ers, meanwhile, opted for a quarterback from Pennsylvania in the third round. He was a signal-caller they scouted who had attended Notre Dame: Joe Montana. In retrospect, that was quite a consolation prize.

• • •

Notre Dame, with its golden dome and heralded Catholic tradition, also became the second home of Bavaro for four years, after he was recruited by Dan Devine to join the Fighting Irish.

An All-American at Danvers (Massachusetts) High School, Bavaro arrived in South Bend in 1981 like many incoming freshmen across the county. "He had been a wild man in high school," Mike Gann, a close friend at school, told the *New York Times*. "Not that he got in trouble; he wasn't like that. He was just a wild-living person. He had long hair, and he had a gut, a big stomach. He was flabby. But after that first semester, he started to change. By his sophomore year, he cut his hair and started to get in shape."

Gann, a former defensive end for the Atlanta Falcons, said he, Bavaro, and fellow freshman Jay Underwood, all of whom played on the football team, hung out together and considered themselves the Three Musketeers.

"Mark doesn't have a false bone in his body. But he's tough to explain; it's tough to put into words what kind of a guy he is," Gann told the newspaper. "He remains cool in a lot of situations, but he opens up to people close to him and rambles on. Sometimes, you can't shut him up."

Gann and Underwood said Bavaro began rounding himself into shape for football, but that he suffered a setback after Notre Dame's first game of his sophomore season, a 23–17 defeat of rival Michigan.

Annoyed at a dorm resident's refusal to let the Three Musketeers in with groceries after hours, Bavaro sliced open his hand breaking a door windowpane. The wound required surgery, caused minor nerve damage in the right thumb, and Bavaro didn't play again that season. The increasingly introspective Bavaro, taken aback by his burst of anger, became the starting tight end as a junior, but was homesick and contemplated quitting after the season to return to Boston.

Bavaro relented after discussions with friends, family, and coaches. He had a terrific senior year, with 32 catches for 395 yards and became an outstanding blocker, a trait that could carry him far into the future. But he had hurt his knee during the season and later underwent arthroscopic surgery on his shoulder. "He plays with pain better than any player I've seen in my 37 years of coaching," Notre Dame coach Gerry Faust declared.

As a result of the injuries and because Bavaro had one season of eligibility left, he slipped to the fourth round of the 1985 draft, where the Giants scooped up the 6'4", 240-pound history major—primarily for his blocking. The Giants had tight end Zeke Mowatt, but with Joe Morris and Maurice Carthon, were a power-running team.

A Smile and a Wink

Ever wonder how a veteran deals with a nervous rookie in a huddle—or what he notices? Here's a revealing comment from former Giants quarterback Kerry Collins in 2003: "I mean, it is different, if you have a rookie coming into the game, it doesn't hurt to crack a joke or give him a little smile and a wink because I've seen guys come in with their eyes as big as saucers," Collins said. "The guys who came in for us were pretty good, they really were kind of calm, I didn't see any signs of 'I'm going to completely lose it.' So you watch and you see and adjust to who comes in at the time."

Bavaro, born nine years after Simms, was on his way to New York to begin what eventually would be a fateful and productive pairing—under the motivational hand of Bill Parcells.

• • •

Given the regal status befitting a first-round draft pick with boyish blond bangs, Simms was dubbed "Prince Valiant" by his new teammates in the 1979 season.

Initially, Simms flourished under his first NFL head coach, Ray Perkins, winning his first four starts and throwing for 1,743 yards and 13 touchdowns. He was voted to the NFL All-Rookie Team.

It would turn out to be the best year in his first five. Simms had more interceptions than touchdown passes (19 to 15) in 1980 and was on his way to better numbers in 1981, but separated his shoulder against the Redskins in a November 15 loss and missed the last five games. The injury would be one in a long line of setbacks for Simms. Scott Brunner replaced Simms, and the Giants won four of the next five to make the playoffs and beat the Eagles in a wild-card game.

In 1982 Simms tore a knee ligament in a preseason game against the Jets and missed the season, which had been slashed to nine games by a players strike. The Giants finished 4–5. Perkins resigned, and defensive coordinator Parcells, whose New Jersey demeanor was an acquired taste, was elevated to head coach.

The team stumbled to a 3–12–1 record in 1983. Brunner foundered, and Simms came in to replace him in the sixth game of the year and fractured his thumb on a helmet while following through on a pass against the Eagles. Nothing was going right.

Until 1984.

Parcells cut dozens of players, had a new training and weight room built, and installed Simms as the starter. He once told him before a game, "If you don't throw two interceptions today, you ain't trying." Simms later realized that Parcells said it "because he didn't want me to be afraid to fail."

Healthy and confident, Simms led the Giants to a playoff spot, passed for 4,044 yards (second most in the NFC) and 22 touchdowns, and was named All-Pro.

In the 1985 season, he would have a new target: Rambo.

· · ·

The biggest box-office smash of the year was *First Blood*, starring Sylvester Stallone as a disgruntled, violent Vietnam crusader who was deployed on search-and-rescue missions: John Rambo. With his resemblance to the *Rocky* star, his toughness, quiet intensity, and the eye-black he wore in games, Bavaro's teammates went for the easy moniker: Rambo. "Hey, First Blood," they joked.

Rambo and Bavaro had one other thing in common: they wouldn't be intimidated.

Bavaro just went about his business and spoke to no one, except for Phil McConkey, the wide receiver and kick returner who was a former Navy pilot. Parcells took note of No. 89, calling him the most impressive rookie in camp.

When the time came for rookie introductions, Bavaro flatly refused to sing the Notre Dame fight song. He also asked his teammates to drop the nickname, believing that he didn't fit the blood-thirsty image and that it was a disrespectful to veterans.

After Mowatt, the starting tight end, suffered a season-ending injury in a exhibition game, Parcells anointed Bavaro as the starter. "He's a stone face," Parcells once remarked on the sideline. "I'd hate to have to fight him."

Two-time All-Pro tight end Mark Bavaro battled through numerous injuries during his six-year Giants career. Photo courtesy of Getty Images

Bavaro had plenty of fight in him. He finished his first NFL season with 37 receptions, 511 yards, and four touchdowns, and earned All-Rookie honors. "I learned from my teammates. I had some pretty good role models to look up to in Harry Carson and Lawrence Taylor and George Martin," said Bavaro.

And he respected Parcells, even though they barely exchanged words. Another time on the sideline, Parcells praised Bavaro for a grab in traffic. "That's a good catch, son," he said. "You've got to learn to beat their hands off you."

Typically low-key and humble, Bavaro just nodded.

Parcells would ride Simms relentlessly as a way to push his buttons, and the quarterback, unlike Bavaro, couldn't resist, and would fire back with expletives. "I said things to Bill that were so cruel and so over the top and so out of place that I couldn't repeat them," Simms recalled. "One curse word after another, horrendously negative, hateful things." But they became friends and admirers after the dust had settled.

"As long as you worked hard for [Parcells], he never had a problem with you," Bavaro said years later. "He can be the greatest guy you could play for or the worst guy you could play for. There are a couple of players he used to coach who are still in therapy because of him."

Beside Bavaro's bullish blocking, the Simms-to-Bavaro connection certainly left some defensive backs and linebackers asking questions and seeking help.

On October 13, Bavaro caught a team-record 12 passes against the Bengals on a day that Simms threw for 513 yards, the fifth-most passing yards in a single game in NFL history.

When the Giants lost 35–30, Bavaro downplayed his performance. "It was nothing special, the plays were the same stuff. I don't know what they did. I just caught a lot of balls. I'd rather win, that's all." The Giants did win—10 games in fact—the most for the team since 1963, and marched into the playoffs. On December 29, Bavaro made five catches, including an 18-yard touchdown and a spectacular one-hander in the 17–3 playoff win over the 'Niners.

Although the Giants were blanked by the Bears 21–0 the following week and ousted from the postseason, Simms ended up passing for 3,829 yards and 22 touchdowns. And he had discovered another go-to guy.

• • •

During the week before a game in October 2003, Patriots head coach Bill Belichick suggested that defensive end Michael Strahan could have started on the famous 1986 Giants.

"He's trying to butter me up," Strahan laughed. "Trying to butter me up, but it's not working; I will be ready to play on Sunday.... Come on, now, apparently they were great without me, great enough to whoop everybody in the league."

Well, not everybody.

With Simms, Bavaro, running back Joe Morris, and all-world linebacker Lawrence Taylor, the 1986 team lost to the Dallas Cowboys by three points in the first game of the year and by five points to the Seattle Seahawks in the seventh week of the season.

But that was it.

Guided by Parcells, who often found himself awash in celebratory Gatorade on the sideline, the Giants steamrolled to a 14–2 regular-season record, won two playoff games by a combined score of 66–3, and wiped out the Denver Broncos in Super Bowl XXI 39–20 for the first Vince Lombardi Trophy in the gilded annals of the franchise.

As the team inched closer to a possible title, each regular-season game was a step on the ladder, with its separate heroics, some special performances, some stories for the archives.

In the season kickoff at Texas Stadium, running back Herschel Walker raised the curtain on his NFL career and provided an opening worthy of Broadway. He gained 64 yards on 10 carries and scored the winning touchdown. The Cowboys led early, but as the offense got on track, the Giants once led by four points in the final quarter in a 31–28 loss.

But the Giants would rebound and win the next five games.

Quarterback Dan Fouts brought the Chargers into the Meadowlands, fresh off scoring 50 points against the Dolphins in Week 1. Not this Sunday. The Giants defense locked San Diego down, pilfering five Fouts passes, two each by Terry Kinard and Kenny Hill. The Chargers running game was stuffed with just 41 yards, and there were seven turnovers in all.

The Giants went west the following week to Los Angeles to face the Raiders. After gaining 83 yards the previous week, Morris broke out with 110 yards, the only time in 19 games that the Raiders had allowed a back to pass the century mark.

Simms threw touchdown passes of 18 and 11 yards to wide receiver Lionel Manuel, and the great back Marcus Allen was smothered with just 40 yards on 15 attempts in a 14–9 win.

Simms needed to generate a comeback in the fourth game in East Rutherford. Down 17–0 to the Saints, the Giants caught a break when linebacker Sam Mills was called for an illegal block on the second-half kickoff that Reuben Mayes brought back 99 yards into the end zone. The offense plodded along until Simms hit Mowatt for a four-yard TD strike that gave Big Blue the lead in the fourth quarter of a 20–17 squeaker.

Bavaro was reported to have a "chipped tooth" afterward, but the man of few words revealed later, before the Super Bowl, that he had a broken jaw that was wired tight for five weeks, so he had to eat food prepared in a blender. "Did it hurt your talking?" someone asked. "Not that anyone noticed," he said.

The defensive battles continued at Busch Stadium in St. Louis.

Simms was off, completing just 8 of 20 for 104 yards—two to Bavaro and two to Bobby Johnson—but the D closed down the Cardinals in a 13–6 snoozer. Morris scored the only touchdown, a one-yarder, in the third. If you liked punting, this one was right up your alley: there were 17 of them.

In the sixth week, the offense and defense put points on the board in a 35–3 rout of the Eagles at Giants Stadium. Taylor ran amok with four sacks of Ron Jaworksi and Randall Cunningham; Carson scored on

Deep Thoughts

Deep thoughts weren't exactly on coach Jim Fassel's mind when kicker Brett Conway missed a field goal in overtime. "The first thing I thought about was when I threw my call sheet up in the air," Fassel admitted. "I thought I would look like a fool if I didn't catch it." When he did, he composed himself and encouraged Conway. "I really thought that he would get another chance. I really did, sincerely I did, and I didn't want him walking over to the bench and sulking."

a pass on a fake field goal; and Simms was 20-for-29, with two touchdown throws, and stepped into the end zone on a rare gallop. The last time the Giants had a similar margin of victory had been five years earlier, a 32–0 whitewash of Seattle.

Naturally, the trap had been set. The 5–1 Giants stepped right in.

The offensive line was paper-thin; Simms was sacked seven times and threw four interceptions against the Seahawks in a 17–12 downer. No one could have guessed at the time, but it would be their final loss of 1986.

While most of New York was tuned in to the seventh and final game of the Mets comeback against the Red Sox in Game 7 of the World Series, over in New Jersey, the Giants got back on track and topped the Redskins 27–20.

Parcells unveiled a new and critical twist: deploying two tight ends, Bavaro and Mowatt, sometimes on the same side of the line. The running attack blossomed; Morris raced for 181 yards and scored the tie-breaking winner on a 13-yard burst with 1:38 to play.

In the rematch with the Cowboys, this time at Giants Stadium, Morris captured the spotlight again, matching his 181 yards of the previous weekend. But the slumping Simms disappointed again, generating just 67 yards on six completions. Thanks to the run-happy offensive line and the defense, however, the Giants won and were 7–2.

At Veterans Stadium in Philly, where the always-nasty fans were rabid, the ugliness spilled over to the field. Players shoved and scrapped; Taylor had three of the club's seven sacks; and Morris put up his fourth consecutive 100-yard game, this time for 111 in a 17–14 win. Several receivers were sidelined with injuries, and Simms only completed one pass to a wideout, 17 yards to backup Solomon Miller. The Eagles, many observers noted, should have won the game.

For Simms, the November 16 game at the Hubert H. Humphrey Metrodome was the personal favorite of his career. "It's everything I always wanted to be as a player," he recalled. "I wanted to be tough, making big throws, immune to pressure, not worried about outcomes. It was truly like standing on the tee box in golf, and there's trees on each side and water, and you just go, 'Man, I'm gonna rip it down the middle.' And no other thought crosses your mind."

The 22–20 escape against the Vikings featured a huge fourth-and-17 completion with 1:12 left in regulation. Down 20–19, with the ball at the Giants 45, the play called was "half-right 74," which aligned three receivers wide: Stacy Robinson split left, Bavaro (who had caught four passes) right, and Johnson. McConkey set up as a flanker on the left but went into motion to the right behind Simms before the snap.

Naturally, the Vikings dropped six defenders back to prevent a killer pass.

Bavaro, sensing a blitz, stayed behind to block. McConkey took off for the end zone, and a trailing Johnson went to the sideline.

Just an instant before Mike Stensrud belted Simms, he lofted the ball over a cornerback to Johnson, who gathered it in at the 30 and danced out of bounds. Raul Allegre's 33-yard field goal provided the margin of victory.

"When Bobby caught the pass, I knew we'd win the game," said Simms. "During the timeout before that, the guys on the Vikings bench had been laughing and joking, confident of victory. They weren't laughing anymore."

Parcells, who had encouraged Simms earlier in the week, chided the press for doubting him. "Anybody who doesn't think Phil Simms is a great quarterback should be covering another sport," Parcells said.

Another huge game-turning play was the main story of the Giants-Broncos match the following week, a pairing that would be revisited in the Super Bowl.

In another tight contest, the Broncos, up 6–3 in the second quarter, were knocking on the door. John Elway had the ball, first-and-10 on the Giants 13.

Elway tried a swing pass to back Gerald Willhite, but defensive end George Martin, the classy elder statesman of the team at age 33, reacted as if he were still on the basketball court at the University of Oregon. He batted Elway's toss in the air, grabbed it, and began to ramble at the 22.

The Broncos pursued, and Elway had an angle on the lumbering Martin at the 35. But Taylor was closing in as well, and Martin deftly faked a lateral to him. Elway lunged, but Martin switched the ball to his left hand and shoved Elway down with his right arm at midfield as the 75,116 at Giants Stadium went wild and the players on the sideline began racing in tandem with Martin, who was being escorted by Taylor and Carson. In the minds of some, this chase involving a Bronco would seem to last as long as the one with the Los Angeles police and O.J. Simpson.

Cornerback Sammy Winder caught up at around the 20, but Mark Collins knocked him to the turf, and Martin, with his last bit of energy, had to hurdle the fallen Bronco at the 15. He plodded into the end zone, where Taylor leapt onto his buddy's back, tackled him from behind, and brought him down in an exhausted, happy heap.

The 78-yard jaunt took 17 seconds.

"When I caught it, it was a bright sunny day," said Martin. "When I got to the end zone, it was cloudy. The weather had changed considerably."

But the temperature would shift again, as Simms needed another long, desperate completion to Johnson—for the second week in a row—on a third-and-21. This catch was for 24 yards and was followed by a 46-yarder to McConkey and an Allegre 34-yard boot for the 19–16 thriller. It was the fifth straight win, and the Giants were rolling. More important, they were beginning to believe.

And Mark Bavaro's signature play, one that defined the toughness and never-say-die resiliency of this squad, was still a week away.

ABC's *Monday Night Football* cameras captured it for posterity.

On December 1, Candlestick Park was the scene of a defining Simms-to-Bavaro moment.

With the Giants trailing 17–0 to Montana and the 49ers in the third quarter, the Giants had the ball a yard across midfield in 'Niners territory. Simms hit Bavaro with a seemingly innocent nine-yard toss over the middle. Bavaro cradled the ball, put his helmet down, and started to churn. Two linebackers bounced off, other defenders grabbed a piece, and finally All-Pro Ronnie Lott flew in and leapt on Bavaro's back.

Bavaro refused to go down and dragged Lott for about 17 yards until four more 49ers converged at the 18 to gang-tackle him. It was a 31-yard infusion of inspiration for the Giants, who scored 21 points in the quarter, the first six coming from a short pass to Morris three plays after Bavaro's gritty catch-and-grind.

The Giants defense, thanks to big run-stuff plays by Gary Reasons and a jolt by Andy Headen that forced Montana to misfire on a final drive, allowed Big Blue to hang on, 21–17.

Naturally, Bavaro dismissed his heroics as "very bad tackling." Few saw it that way. None other than coach Bill Walsh later called Bavaro the premier tight end in the league. Not that any of this acclaim fazed Bavaro, who would finish the season with 66 catches, snapping the Giants' record for receptions by a tight end held by Bob Tucker with 59. The 23-year-old racked up 1,001 yards and four touchdowns, made the Pro Bowl, and still strolled around in jeans and sneakers, drove a Chevy, and lived in a hotel not far from Giants Stadium.

"Mark is very intelligent and he's also very gentle, although I don't suppose the 49ers would agree with that," said Simms.

At RFK Stadium in Washington, Bavaro caught one of three touchdowns against the Redskins as the Giants climbed to 12–2 and first place in the NFC East. Simms threw other TDs to Johnson and McConkey, Taylor had three more sacks, and the attacking defense picked off hapless Jay Schroeder six times in the 24–14 win.

Against the Cardinals at home, the defense set a franchise record with nine sacks, and Morris, who had rushed for just 81 yards against the Redskins, gobbled up 179 and three scores. Simms had an below-average day, but the Giants collected 251 yards on the ground in the 27–7 victory.

The regular season concluded in New Jersey with a bang as the Giants secured home-field advantage in the playoffs with their ninth straight win, a 55–24 demolition of the Packers. That tied their mark of nine set in 1962.

The game set the tone for a remarkable postseason, a year in which Taylor, with 20.5 sacks, became the only defensive player to win the league MVP unanimously. He, Bavaro, Morris, Carson, Leonard Marshall, guard Brad Benson, nose tackle Jim Burt, and punter Sean Landeta were named as Pro Bowlers, and Parcells was selected Coach of the Year.

•   •   •

January 1987. How times have changed. The Beastie Boys were the first act to be censored by *American Bandstand*. The Dow closed above 2,000 for the first time. And *Return to Horror High*, a cheesy movie that had George Clooney in about two scenes, was in theaters.

The 49ers starred in their own version of *Horror High* at Giants Stadium on January 3.

The nightmare began on San Francisco's first possession at midfield. Montana threw a short slant to future Hall of Fame wideout Jerry Rice—generally one of the surest plays in the NFL. Rice cradled the ball and took off. He was in the clear and racing for a score when he inexplicably fumbled the ball off his knee at the 26, tried to recover while slowing down, but deflected it into the end zone, where Giants safety Kenny Hill, pursuing from behind, recovered. The stunned 'Niners wouldn't cross the goal line again.

Simms capped the ensuing 80-yard drive by zipping a 24-yard touchdown to Bavaro. Morris ran for 100 yards in the first half behind an offensive line that Parcells had needled all week as "Club 13"—referring to the abysmal 13 yards rushing the Giants had generated in the regular season against the 'Niners. Change that to "Club 159," which was Morris' final yardage. Courtesy of a 45-yard Morris run, the scoreboard read 14–3 Giants.

The rout was just beginning. Again, Bavaro was part of a series of big plays. Late in the second quarter, on a fourth-and-6 at the San Francisco 28, Parcells dipped into his bag of tricks for a fake field goal.

Holder Jeff Rutledge surprised the defense, shouting "Shift!" and kicker Raul Allegre lined up wide left, outside Bavaro, drawing coverage. Bavaro was left to single-coverage by a linebacker. He caught Rutledge's throw for 23 yards, down to the 5.

Simms went back in and hit Johnson in the end zone, but was pile-driven into the ground by Dwaine Board and left the field dizzy. Naturally, his teammates were concerned.

"The most Mark's ever talked to me," Simms said later, "was when I got hit pretty hard in that game, and he asked me, 'Are you all right?' I figured this guy must really like me."

After the kickoff, Montana wouldn't like nose guard Jim Burt very much.

Burt, an emotional player, came to the Giants as an undrafted free agent back in 1981 and enjoyed a love-hate relationship with Parcells, who once said that Burt "runs two quarts low."

In practice, Parcells often made the nose guard lift a 50-pound dumbbell repeatedly off the ground to simulate bringing his arm up powerfully out of his stance at the snap to hammer linemen. And it was Burt, in 1985, who began the tradition of drenching Parcells with a barrel of Gatorade on the sideline after a win.

With time running down in the half, Montana dropped back to pass, looking for Rice. Burt came up the middle and unloaded on Montana, who went flying backward, landing on his helmet and sustaining a concussion. The fluttering ball was grabbed by Taylor, who sprinted into the end zone for a 28–3 lead at halftime.

Montana was finished for the day, and so were the 'Niners. "It was clean, but I don't feel good about it," said Burt, who would be limited by severe back problems and told by the Giants to retire two years later.

True to form, Burt didn't quit and would later sign with the 49ers and win a second Super Bowl ring—a year before the Giants would have their second piece of championship jewelry.

In the second half, the Giants' dominance continued. Morris would score again, Simms would throw two more TD passes, and the defense was stifling. Overall, it held the 49ers to 29 yards rushing, 184 yards in total offense, and nine first downs.

"That was just a good ol' fashioned ass-whupping," Taylor chortled after the game. Asked if Rice scoring early rather than fumbling would have made a difference in the game, he shot back: "Yeah, the final score would have been 49–10."

The 1985 Bears had been the NFL's poster boys, and the 15–2 Giants had hoped for a chance to topple the defending champs, who had bounced them from the postseason a year ago, 21–0 at Soldier Field.

This year, the Giants would host the first NFC title game on their home turf in the New Jersey swamps. But the Redskins had ousted the Bears in the other conference semifinal, and Washington was the opponent on January 11.

Instead, the Windy City was in the Meadowlands, with gusts of up to 30 mph, of which the Bill Belichick–designed defense made the most. The Giants chose the wind at their back after winning the coin flip, and the 'Skins couldn't get rolling. Punts and passes went awry, and Allegre, with the wind, made a 47-yarder for a 3–0 lead. Simms welcomed back Lionel Manuel, in uniform the first time in 10 weeks following an injury, with two passes, including a touchdown off a scramble for a 10–0 lead. It was all the Giants would need.

But the Simms-to-Bavaro combo would have another impact play. A catch-and-run brought the ball to the Redskins 10, where Simms almost scored on a bootleg. He faked a handoff right and took off around the left side, where he trudged to the 1-foot line. A Chris Godfrey block allowed Morris to curl around the right side for the 17–0 lead.

Taylor sat out much of the second half, as sacks of Jay Schroeder (20-for-50 passing) by Erik Dorsey and Leonard Marshall blunted drives. In the end, Carson chased Parcells with the Gatorade bucket, and the coach feinted a few times before the inevitable dousing. Amid confetti blowing in the chilly breeze, Parcells was carried off the field.

The Giants had knocked off the 'Skins three times in one season, and for the first time in 23 years, they were close to the summit of the NFL's grandest mountain.

Next stop, Pasadena.

• • •

On the Thursday after the Redskins game, the Giants reported for practice at the Meadowlands.

Center Bart Oates described it as "lackluster, mediocre," and players said Parcells was steamed, saying, "This won't do. You've got to pick it up."

The next day, Simms was razor-sharp, connecting on every bullet. "Hey, save something for the game," Parcells said. According to Paul Zimmerman of *Sports Illustrated*, "Phil had this strange sort of a glow. It was like he was in a perfect biorhythm stage or something."

There was running and more running, 60- and 100-yard sprints. Did they complain? Players said no, coaches thought differently. Said Johnny Parker, the strength and conditioning coach, "Listen, these guys would complain if you made them run six five-yarders."

The longest, most intimidating practice came on the Monday before the game: Oates recalled it as one of the three or four hardest of the year, and Wednesday in the heat, Parcells pressed the pedal down even further with the drills and the verbal drilling.

Brad Benson was one of the whipping boys.

The massive left tackle from Penn State had several run-ins with Parcells, with one explosive incident that players particularly remember. In the Vikings game, Allegre booted a 55-yard field goal as time expired in the second quarter. But Benson was whistled for an illegal motion penalty, negating the kick and moving the ball back five yards. Allegre missed; Parcells freaked.

Benson recalled, "I could read his lips on the sideline. It wasn't pretty. There were words there that would set just about anybody off." The two started moving toward each other, but George Martin grabbed Parcells, and Carson restrained Benson. A truce was forged on the plane after the win, but the message had been sent.

And another was sent on that Wednesday. "Benson," Parcells shouted, "you're going to be famous on Sunday for all of the wrong reasons!"

It was all part of Parcells' maniacal motivation.

"We all knew what Bill was doing, the way he was driving us," Burt said later. "I thought he'd lost his mind when he had us in half pads…shoulder pads and shorts…and then ran a lot of interior line work. I wound up with bruises all over my legs. I almost got into a couple of fights out there. I mean, I was that far away from going after Karl Nelson and even Leonard Marshall on my own unit. But it paid off, didn't it? We were in the right mood. All the running got us in shape. We finished the game strong."

Despite the accolades for quarterback John Elway, the Giants were favored by nine points in Super Bowl XXI on January 25. "Ludicrous," Parcells declared.

"I don't ever think about betting lines," said guard Chris Godfrey. "We beat them once and we know we can beat them again, but we also know John Elway is good enough of a quarterback to beat anyone. So how can you make sense with a betting line?"

After all, Elway was hot. He led the Broncos to this game at the Rose Bowl by defeating the Cleveland Browns on a famous series at the end of the fourth quarter that became known as "the Drive." In 5:02, Elway's

Broncos marched 98 yards to tie the game with 37 seconds left in regulation and won in overtime.

But for the season, Elway's and Simms' stats were eerily similar. Elway had 3,485 yards passing and 19 touchdowns. Simms had thrown for 3,487 yards and 21 touchdown passes, but had been inconsistent in the playoffs, just 9-for-19 against the 'Niners and 7-for-14 against Washington.

But Simms, benched, booed, and beset by injuries in his eight-year career, sensed something special on that Sunday. Godfrey, Benson, and Simms grabbed a taxi about five hours before kickoff. Benson was nervous and asked Simms how he felt. "'Not nervous,' he said, 'excited,'" according to Benson. "Then he said, 'I'm telling you guys, I feel great. I'm gonna be throwing some fastballs today. Give me time, and I'll rip 'em.'"

Even during warmups in front of a crowd of 101,063 in Pasadena, Simms said later, "I coasted. I went at half speed. I wasn't even dropping back. I felt that I had good rhythm, and I didn't want to mess with it…. Right from the first day of practice, I felt that I was going to have a good game. I felt good about throwing the ball. Conditions were just perfect for passing. I could see that the ball was carrying better. The weather was great. I was used to throwing in the cold, but now I could grip the ball any way I wanted to. I could make it do anything I wanted."

And he did.

In spectacular, one-for-the-ages fashion.

In the first quarter, however, Elway was doing his thing too. He found Mark Jackson for 24 yards on a third-and-7 against the Giants' vaunted defense and Rich Karlis' field-goal bid sailed between the uprights from 48 yards. Denver 3, Giants 0.

Simms went to work, and a six-yard toss, not to Bavaro but to the Giants' other tight end, Zeke Mowatt, concluded a 78-yard campaign for a 7–3 edge.

Elway, whose running ability (he had 257 yards rushing in 1986) set him apart from some other strong-armed quarterbacks of the era, restored the Denver lead when he darted in from four yards out on a quarterback draw.

The Broncos' defense was charging, rushing four attackers, but the offensive line responded. Simms executed some pretty play-action passes to keep the rush off back Joe Morris.

"They changed their whole offensive attack," Broncos linebacker Karl Mecklenburg said. "Pass first, run second. It surprised us. We thought they would try to establish the running game, but they went against their tendencies, and they did a good job of it."

Simms completed all nine first-down passes in the first half to keep the Broncos off-balance. On the only third-and-long, he connected with Stacy Robinson on the sideline for 18 yards.

"We practiced all week head up, butt down, keep your feet moving," Oates said. "Stay light on your feet and play patty-cake with them. No firing out. Passive-type blocking."

Only when the Broncos blitzed did they have success. Safety Dennis Smith's rushes prompted two of the three incompletions Simms threw all day.

The scrambling Elway, meanwhile, was matching Simms for accuracy. In the first 15 minutes, they were 13-for-13 combined. Elway's deepest successes were 54 yards to Vance Johnson and 31 yards to Steve Watson.

Parcells contended that he had been prepared for the way things unfolded, and had spoken to the defensive players before the game. "I told them not to worry about him getting completions early and making plays," he recalled. "Keep wearing them down. Just don't let the receivers turn into runners. After a while, we'll make some plays, or they'll run out of room."

In the second quarter, the defense rose up to wall off the Broncos in a mighty goal-line stand that turned the course of the game. With a chance to extend the 10–7 lead, the Broncos had a first down on the Giants 1-yard line.

More Colorado beef arrived in the form of an extra tackle and tight end, but Taylor and nose tackle Erik Howard corralled Elway for a one-yard loss. Carson nailed running back Gerald Willhite for no gain. On third down, the Giants used some photographic memory.

Watching film of the previous matchup during the week, linebacker Carl Banks had seen the Broncos pitch out for a score from four yards out. "I expected that play again," Banks said, "and that's what they called."

Banks read the flip to Sammy Winder, and he, Carson, and cornerback Perry Williams crunched Winder for a four-yard loss. "I didn't have time to square up.... I just got my head in there and made the hit," Banks, who had 10 tackles in the game, said later. "I had zigzags in my eyes for the rest of the half."

Karlis missed the 23-yard field-goal try. Uh-oh.

Four chances from 36 inches: no points.

After a Giants punt, Martin—the eldest Giant at 33, who had batted down an Elway pass and made a long 78-yard return for a TD in the regular season—didn't have to run anywhere near as far this time. He sacked Elway for a safety to cut the lead to 10–9.

The Broncos, abandoning the run because the Giants had held their backs to just 14 yards, rode back downfield to the 16 on Elway's arm. But the Giants were fortunate—the saying is that you need some luck to win—and Karlis' luck was bad. During the year, Karlis had been 11-for-12 from 39 yards or less, but he shanked the ball wide again, from 34.

The Giants escaped and would run away from the Broncos in the second half, starting with some more Parcells gambits.

On the opening drive in the third quarter, the Giants set up to punt from their 44. Backup quarterback Jeff Rutledge shifted out of the formation, took the snap, and gained two yards for a first down. Five plays later, it was Simms...to Bavaro...touchdown. Thirteen yards and a lead, 16–10, that they would not lose.

"I probably should not have thrown it, but I saw this little opening [in double coverage]," Simms said.

Bavaro genuflected in the end zone and motioned the sign of the cross. "It wasn't premeditated," Bavaro said. "I was very grateful and thankful at the time. I'm grateful every time I walk off the football field and I'm healthy and I've made it through another series. I kneel and give thanks to God in every area of my life. It wasn't anything special. It was very routine, kneeling down in the Super Bowl, because that's what I do in my life. It wasn't a show. It wasn't an act."

The touchdown ignited the biggest offensive fireworks display in one half in Super Bowl history. Simms went 10-for-10 as the Giants scored four touchdowns and a field goal on the first five possessions.

For the Giants, the real difference-maker wasn't the Karlis misses or the Bavaro catch. It was another gadget play that turned out to be Simms' longest completion of the day, 44 yards to Phil McConkey, off a flea-flicker that set up the Giants' second touchdown of the second half. From left end, McConkey went in motion, and Simms handed off to Morris, who took two steps and flipped the pigskin back to Simms. Bobby Johnson was wide open down the sideline, but Simms didn't see him. Instead, he glimpsed McConkey cutting across the middle from right to left toward that same sideline. McConkey caught the ball at the 20 and was upended at the 1-yard line by cornerback Mark Haynes, but the damage was done, the play a killer.

Morris bulled in on the next down, and with 24 seconds left in the third quarter, with the Broncos beginning to wither in the 76-degree heat, the end of the rainbow was in sight.

"We ran the flea-flicker in practice for I don't know how long, and we never hit the damn thing," said Simms. "When I hit McConkey, I thought, *That's it. We've won it.*"

The Simms-to-Bavaro saga didn't end there. Actually, it was Simms-to-Bavaro-to-McConkey that was indicative of the way the Giants' fortunes had ascended.

The Giants were up 26–10, and Simms' last pass of the day—as it turned out—was high to Bavaro in the end zone from six yards out. Bavaro reached up, was hit by two Broncos, and the ball glanced backward off his fingertips.

Waiting was McConkey—"watching the ball come down in slow-motion," he would recall—and he gathered it in about a foot from the ground. An exuberant Bavaro—who remains close friends with McConkey—lifted him toward the California night sky.

It was a fitting end for Simms' nearly perfect night. He completed 22 of 25 passes (two of his three incompletions were drops by receivers) for 268 yards and three touchdowns, setting Super Bowl records for consecutive completions (10), accuracy (88 percent), and passer rating

Phil McConkey celebrates his fourth-quarter touchdown in Super Bowl XXI with teammate Mark Bavaro. Photo courtesy of Getty Images

(158.3). "He quarterbacked as good a game as ever has been played," said Parcells. "Technically as close to a perfect game as I've seen a quarterback have," said the Giants' offensive coordinator, Ron Erhardt.

The 30 second-half points in the 39–20 victory set a Super Bowl record for points in a half, and Simms was named MVP. The record for completion percentage in a postseason game was broken by the New England Patriots' Tom Brady in a January 2008 AFC Divisional Playoff game, but Simms' mark stands as a Super Bowl record.

"We threw everything we had at them," said Elway, who passed for a more-than-respectable 304 yards. "I thought I did everything I could do." Mecklenberg didn't blame the distraught Karlis: "The way the Giants moved the ball in the second half, six points wouldn't have made a difference."

Yes, the 1985 Bears, who went 18–1 under Mike Ditka and had glamour and personality and talent with Walter Payton, Mike Singletary, Jim McMahon, and Richard Dent, as well as the "Super Bowl Shuffle" video, deserved all the accolades and will go down in NFL history as one of the greatest teams.

But the 17–2 Giants, who powered through the playoffs, scoring 105 points and surrendering just 23, are at least in the conversation. The opening-day loss was with an out-of-shape Taylor, who had the most dominant season by a defensive player in NFL history. And the Giants dispatched the Redskins, who would win the following Super Bowl, and the Broncos, who would appear in three of the next four Super Bowls.

And Simms outplayed Elway.

The Gatorade bath that Burt had initiated in 1985 punctuated the evening. Carson soaked Parcells in the final minutes of the game, and Simms—who was named MVP and was the first one credited with saying the sponsored postgame phrase "I'm going to Disneyland"—was wet as well. Benson and Oates, who had protected him in his finest hour, supplied the ice-water baptism.

"I think it was very appropriate to cool the guy down," Oates said, "as hot as he was in the game."

•   •   •

After the 1986 Super Bowl, Simms' NFL career cooled, although he became a respected television analyst. Bavaro played in and won another Super Bowl in 1990, before a degenerative knee condition forced him to quit the game in 1995 at age 32.

The next image of Bavaro after the vanquishing of the Broncos came when he appeared on the cover or *Sports Illustrated*'s NFL preview issue for the 1987 season. Kneeling with his pads over his shoulder, Bavaro was pictured under a caption: "The Living End: Mark Bavaro of the New York Giants."

He was married that season, which finished with another Pro Bowl after 55 receptions for 867 yards and eight touchdowns. In 1988 he snagged 53 balls for 672 yards and four touchdowns.

Bavaro's secular life sometimes intermingled with his religious one. Bavaro was one of 503 people arrested and released during a pro-life rally in 1988, and he continued his Catholic-based activities long after.

In 1990 Bavaro missed practices because of his knee, yet made two critical third-down catches in Super Bowl XXV against the Bills in the 20–19 win. But the proud, quiet man who had played through so many injuries was betrayed by that knee. Doctors, including the one who advised the Giants, suggested that Bavaro retire. The stubborn Bavaro refused and was cut in July 1991, but later was given a $310,000 contract and placed on the PUP (physically unable to perform) list by the team.

He was recruited by a friend as a tight ends coach at Saint Dominic Savio High School in East Boston, and he spent the winter in that role. Yet the pangs of feeling that his playing days had not ended were there. In 1992 former Giants assistant Bill Belichick signed him to a deal in Cleveland. He played one season for the Browns, then two more for the Eagles, and was still a formidable target, with 43 receptions for 481 yards and six touchdowns in 1993. His career numbers over nine seasons were exceptional: 351 receptions for 4,733 yards and 39 touchdowns.

Despite it all, he remained a Giant at heart. "I don't ever think of myself as an Eagle," he said. But he always thought of himself as a writer, and in 2008 *Rough and Tumble*, a fictional account of his days in the league, was published.

Hello, Security? We Have an Issue...

Maybe some coaches should wear name tags.

In the summer of 1990, the Giants were in the beginning of training camp at Fairleigh Dickinson in Madison, New Jersey. Mark Bavaro, a Notre Dame grad, and his teammates were chilling outside the cafeteria when a heavyset guy with a Jersey accent approached the legendary tight end. "This guy starts asking me about Notre Dame," Bavaro said. "I had never seen Charlie [Weis] before. I didn't know he was a coach. I thought. *Who is this guy and how did he get over here?* I was ready to get security."

And as he has grown, Bavaro hasn't been as shy in his opinions. When Jeremy Shockey, the rebellious, mouthy, and demonstrative tight end joined the Giants in 2002 and made a splash in the New York tabloids, Bavaro—old-school forever—derided the new-school attitude. "He [Shockey] makes a routine catch and gives the first-down signal," Bavaro said. "That's the game today. I sound like an old fogey.... He probably could conserve a lot of energy post-play and get back to the huddle."

Like Bavaro, Shockey often played hurt, but that's where the stylistic line ended.

"I was kind of an extra lineman. Bill [Parcells] tried to move me and do stuff Shockey does a lot. I didn't like it," Bavaro told interviewers. "I didn't think I was very good at it. He seems to be more comfortable away from the line, although he plays that in-tight tight end well. He certainly does not shy away from contact. That's what you need to be a good blocker. He's sneaky effective."

From afar, the acerbic Parcells weighed in, and staunchly commended his former player. "You want to start comparing him [Shockey] to Bavaro?" asked Parcells. "Put a defensive end in front of him and tell everybody you're going to run over there, and let's see if he can knock him back four yards and you can make 12 yards. Then you can compare him to Bavaro. 'Til then, I don't want to hear it."

For Simms, the year after the Super Bowl was a drop-off, but the next two were progressions. In 1987 he registered the second-highest quarterback rating in the NFC, throwing for 2,230 yards, 17 touchdowns, and only nine interceptions. The 1988 season was far better, though, when the Giants finished 10–6 but lost a shot at the playoff in a tiebreaker. Simms recorded 3,359 yards passing and 21 touchdowns, completing 54.9 percent of his attempts.

"Parcells once took me aside and told me how disappointed he was in me," Simms recalled. "He said, 'You used to be a leader but now you are trying to be everyone's friend.'" In 1989 Simms and the Giants took few prisoners, finished 12–4, and Simms passed for 3,061 yards but struggled with costly turnovers near the end of the season, when he misfired for several of his 14 interceptions. The favored Giants also dropped a playoff game at home against the Los Angeles Rams, 19–13.

In the off-season, Simms was hobbled by an ankle injury, but was looking forward to 1990, having seen the team that was assembled. So the resilient Simms would stage a comeback—albeit it one that ended bitterly—in 1990. He directed the Giants to an 11–3 record, and a shot at another ring, another chance to perform in the NFL's biggest arena, certainly seemed feasible.

That quest ended abruptly.

Lineman Leon Seals of the Bills—whom the Giants would later face in Super Bowl XXV—sacked him on a scramble for no gain in that 14th game, and Simms broke his foot. He was done for the year.

The injury made backup Jeff Hostetler the starter, and he—along with a magnificent defense—carried the Giants to the Super Bowl against those Bills. Simms, like other injured players, was distanced from the core of the team.

In Tampa during the Super Bowl festivities, Simms was asked about the 1986 game. "I've thought about that game 700 times since I got here," Simms said. "It was special, beyond special. It's going to be one of the highlights of my life. It's more than football. I'm very grateful for it."

He made it clear to writers that he was discouraged, but accepted the inevitable: not being a part of meetings, strategy, the spotlight. "There are players and the people who back them up and the people who are hurt," Simms said. "I've been hurt before. Before this injury, I was walking out of the locker room one day when I saw Adrian White and Odessa Turner and Raul Allegre, and I was thinking, 'They're hurt and not part of the team.' It's not easy. Sitting and watching is tough." Especially in games that really count.

"There was not a lot of satisfaction in the season I had," the fiercely competitive Simms declared. "I thought I played very well. I did what I was supposed to do. But if you're on a good team, nothing matters except the playoffs. The playoffs are a whole different thing."

Asked about a possible retirement, Simms was defiant. "I promise you I won't retire gracefully," he said. Nor did he gracefully accept what happened next.

Hostetler and the Giants edged the Bills 20–19 in the Super Bowl when Scott Norwood's potential game-winning kick sailed wide.

Simms' mentor, Parcells, resigned and was replaced by running backs coach Ray Handley. One of Handley's first decisions was to name Hostetler as the starter, a decision that made Simms, well, simmer.

The team struggled, and it wasn't until the 13th game of the season that Simms regained the job, and that was only because Hostetler had broken a bone in his back against Tampa Bay in the previous game. The Giants finished 8–8.

Simms would keep the number-one spot the next season, but was injured early in the year and was sidelined for the duration. The Giants faded to a 6–10 record, and Handley was fired. In those two years, Simms had played in just 10 games. It certainly appeared that at age 38, his long career was coming to a close.

However, Simms found new football life. Former Broncos coach Dan Reeves was installed as head coach, and he immediately released Hostetler and named Simms the team's starting quarterback. He started all 16 games in 1993, one of only seven NFL quarterbacks to do so, and guided the revived Giants to an 11–5 season and a victory over the Minnesota Vikings in the playoffs.

But injury struck again: he tore a labrum and underwent shoulder surgery after the season. Simms was expected to be ready in time for training camp but, with the team handicapped by salary-cap issues, was later released and chose to retire.

During the onset of the "show me the money" era of free agency, Simms was one of the few great players to remain on the same team for his entire career—14 years. In those 14 seasons with the Giants, Simms completed 2,576 of 4,647 passes for 33,462 yards and 199 touchdowns. Those 33,000-plus yards rank No. 20 in NFL history. Not the fleetest of foot, he nonetheless had 349 carries for 1,252 yards and six touch-downs.

Although he may eventually be surpassed by Eli Manning, when he retired, Simms held team records for most passes completed and attempted in one game (40 and 62), season (286/533), and career (2,576/4,647), most career touchdown passes (199), and most 300-yard games in a career (21). In August 2001 *Sports Illustrated* proclaimed Simms the "Most Underrated Quarterback" in NFL history.

Simms' arm had one last throw in him. On September 4, 1995, his jersey was retired in a halftime ceremony of a game in Giants Stadium against the Dallas Cowboys, and it provided an unexpected twist to Simms' career. During his emotional speech, Simms stated that he wanted to put the No. 11 on one last time, and throw one final pass, this one to teammate Lawrence Taylor. "All of a sudden it kind of hit me," Simms said later. "I've put Lawrence in a really tough spot—national TV, he's got dress shoes and a sports jacket on, and he's had a few beers, and he's going to run down the field, and I'm going to throw him a pass."

Simms motioned for the nervous Taylor to run a longer pattern, and after about 30 yards, threw him the ball. "I'm saying to myself, *If I drop this pass, I got to run my black ass all the way to Upper Saddle River, because there ain't no way I'm going to be able to stay in that stadium,*" the always-irreverent Taylor said with a laugh.

Taylor managed to hang on, and the Giants faithful lustily voiced their approval.

Simms, of course, never went far from the game in which he prospered.

After his retirement, he was wooed by NBC to join its lead broad-cast crew. He teamed with Dick Enberg and Paul Maguire on the cover-age of Super Bowl XXX and Super Bowl XXXII. Simms went to CBS in 1998, teaming first with Greg Gumbel and then with Jim Nantz on the lead broadcast team, and the transition has been seamless.

In his game analysis and in interviews, Simms remains plainspoken. Never has he forgotten his past and what it brought him. Especially one incredible performance in Pasadena.

"Look at the two New York quarterbacks, Joe Namath and myself," Simms said. "We've done a lot with one damn game. That's just the truth.... Playing well and winning the Super Bowl helped my credibility.

Otherwise, when I'd give an opinion [on television], people would say, 'What has he done?' If I didn't win that Super Bowl, I'd probably be coaching somewhere. TV would not be an option for me. Winning a Super Bowl gives you a bigger chip in the game, and people perceive you to be better than you are. It gives you a stronger voice in the game."

Nor has he forgotten the connection with one particular receiver.

Asked if he had a choice to pick a play-by-play man to work one last Super Bowl broadcast, the still-blond Simms said: "I'd do it with Pat Summerall."

Why?

"I can still hear his calls in my sleep: "Simms…Bavaro… Touchdown."

chapter 3

Climbing Back to the Top: 1990

We all tend to edit our young lives to our children, otherwise a lot of us would horrify them to a point where they would wonder what they were doing with such crazy parents. I told [my son Zak] what made some of those Giants teams special and why they were capable of winning a Super Bowl when there were probably two, three, maybe four teams out there that were more talented. The kind of individuals that we had on those teams were guys that would work so hard and that would do everything and anything at all to win a football game. The type of guys that just loved to play and loved to compete. I couldn't speak for the 1986 team, they were an outstanding team, but that 1990 team was a bunch of guys that just wouldn't hide and found ways to get the job done. If a slow, fat, short, white linebacker like myself could contribute to that team, then you know something is special about it.

—Linebacker Steve DeOssie

Spurred to Victory

The bitter memory of the final game of the 1989 season had been burned into the minds of the Giants. In overtime of a divisional playoff game, Rams wide receiver Flipper Anderson caught the game-winning touchdown pass over cornerback Mark Collins, sped down the sideline, through the end zone, and straight into the tunnel that led to the locker rooms, casting a pall on the crowd at Giants Stadium.

And the hangover stretched into the 1990 preseason. After a league suspension and rehab for cocaine addiction had somewhat tamed his wild life, perennial All-Pro linebacker Lawrence Taylor held out for 44 days before the season. The Giants offered him $1.2 million a year; he wanted $3 million, more than the Eagles' Reggie White. They settled at $7.5 million for three years, the largest pact ever for a defensive player.

In the opener, LT started afresh against the Eagles and finished with three sacks and a forced fumble in a 27–20 win, as the defense, which would be a major storyline all season, limited the Eagles to 81 rushing yards. The Giants dominated the Cowboys on the broiling artificial turf at Texas Stadium in Week 2, 28–7, as Taylor intercepted a Troy Aikman pass and returned it for a touchdown.

The Cowboys' rushing yards? Twenty.

Giants center Bart Oates still felt the Giants offense could improve. "We missed a lot of assignments," he said. "We rushed the ball okay, but not like we did in preseason. Phil [Simms] was pressured some. There were plenty of things we didn't do."

And so it went, first a 20–3 dispatching of the Dolphins and then a 31–17 rout of the hated Cowboys, both at Giants Stadium. The offense perked up, with Simms firing scoring passes to Mark Ingram, Rodney Hampton, and Bob Mrosko, and backup Jeff Hostetler scampering for a 12-yard touchdown in the fourth quarter. A bye week didn't derail the Giants Express, although they just eked by the Redskins the following week, 24–20, in Washington.

The score was much closer against Phoenix in East Rutherford, and a comeback from being down 19–10 was required in the final 5:38. Hostetler found Stephen Baker for a 38-yard touchdown, and a 40-yard field goal by Matt Bahr won it 20–19. "It wasn't pretty," said Taylor. "But you don't ask how to win, you just win." Hostetler, Baker, Bahr, and of course Taylor, would all be heard from much more in this intriguing season.

To improve to 7–0, all three scores against Washington at home were set up by interceptions: two by cornerback Everson Walls (one of which he returned for six) and one by Greg Jackson. The final: 21–10.

By now, the pattern had emerged. Opposing offenses were being stifled, and the Giants would dominate ball-possession and not turn it over, outdoors or indoors. The team would end the year with an NFL record for fewest turnovers: 14.

At the Hoosier Dome, the Big Blue defense held Jeff George and the Colts to 11 first downs, 181 total yards, and 55 rushing yards. Simms completed 17 of 21 for 172 yards, and his lone interception ended a streak of 150 passes without one. Defensive end Leonard Marshall sacked George twice.

Revenge against the Rams in California was next. Simms was accurate and efficient in a 31–7 trouncing. Beating the Detroit Lions the following week would give the franchise its best start ever at 10–0. It was hardly suspenseful. Ingram caught a 57-yard pass from Simms, and it was 17–0 in the second quarter. A field goal made it 20–0, and the second half was scoreless. Coach Bill Parcells' comment was priceless: "The offense played well when I let them. We didn't do anything stupid."

Actually, the Giants defense was particularly bright. In those 10 wins, they had surrendered seven points or less five times.

The offense, however, continued to struggle, scoring just 13 in the first loss of the season, 31–13 to the Eagles. In a game marked by scuffles as the Giants' frustration mounted, the Eagles piled up 405 yards and scored two touchdowns in 22 seconds in the fourth quarter. Quarterback Randall Cunningham, who would be voted the league's Most Valuable Player, rushed for 66 yards and completed 17 of 31 passes for 229 yards. Taylor was held to one tackle.

In a 7–3 loss to the 49ers the next week, tempers boiled over again. The Giants held Jerry Rice to one catch for 13 yards, but couldn't score themselves. After San Francisco, whose defense, led by ferocious Charles Haley, foiled four straight Simms pass attempts in the fourth quarter with the ball on the 9-yard line, Simms and safety Ronnie Lott chirped at each other.

By Week 14, Taylor had seen enough. He delivered fiery, emotional speeches and backed them up with 12 tackles and 2.5 sacks of Vikings quarterback Rich Gannon in a 23–15 win. "He told us, 'I'm going to start playing the way we're supposed to play. If anybody wants to come along, fine,'" DeOssie said. "He changed our attitude."

Jeff Hostetler went from backup quarterback to Super Bowl hero in 1990–1991.

After beating the Vikings, however, the Giants lost to the Bills 17–13 in the final regular-season home game, and in a troubling turn of events, Simms was knocked out for the season with a broken foot.

The focus of the offense had to change with Hostetler, who had thrown just 93 passes in his NFL career, and Parcells and his staff designed plays to capitalize on his scrambling ability.

In the 24–21 win over the Cardinals—one of the weaker teams in the league—Hostetler threw for 191 yards and ran for 31 in his first start. The Giants defense sagged through the game, allowing 381 yards in the air from quarterback Timm Rosenbach, but held on. Two of the

Cardinals' fourth-quarter drives resulted in interceptions, and their final drive was stopped by a Taylor sack.

Going into the last game, the Giants had a chance to clinch the No. 2 seed in the playoffs. In Foxboro, against a Patriots team that had lost 13 in a row, the season finale should have been a breeze. It wasn't. But Hostetler proved his worth.

Hostetler ran for 82 of the team's season-high 213 yards, but the Pats almost tied the game at 13 in the fourth quarter. Jason Staurovsky missed a 42-yard field goal, Hostetler then ran a 30-yard bootleg on a third down, and the Giants ran out the clock on a surprisingly successful season.

Postseason Revenge

The season-long formula was tweaked against the longtime rival Chicago Bears in the postseason game at Giants Stadium on January 13. Parcells and defensive coordinator Bill Belichick used a four-man defensive line most of the game—as opposed to their usual 3-4—a formation that ruffled the Bears' blocking assignments. Running back Neal Anderson was suffocated; he was held to a season-low 19 yards on 12 carries. Bears quarterback Mike Tomczak was 17-for-36 passing for 205 yards and tossed two interceptions in the 31–3 loss.

Two other key elements remained: Ottis Anderson rushed for 80 of the team's 194 yards on 21 carries as the Giants once again controlled the ball for 38:22, almost two-thirds of the game.

But all that was prelude. The next two games would be among the most legendary in the history of the club that Tim Mara bought for $500 in 1925.

On January 20, some tickets were being scalped for $500 outside of Candlestick Park for the chance to see the two-time defending champion 49ers take another step toward a Super Bowl three-peat in this, the NFC Championship Game.

The 'Niners had won seven consecutive postseason games, and Joe Montana was ready for number eight. A capacity crowd of 65,750 squeezed into the windy park on the bay and watched the sides trade field goals in the first and second quarter for a 6-all tie at halftime.

So, as was the case in so many huge battles in so many decades of pro football, the game would be decided on big plays in the second half. Who could make them?

With about five minutes gone in the third quarter, Montana finally struck gold. He threw a 61-yard touchdown pass to wide receiver John Taylor to give his men a 13–6 lead.

Against many defenses, that might have been enough to jump-start the dangerous 49ers offense the rest of the way. But it would be their last points of the day. The Giants allowed just five first downs through the next 25 minutes.

"That was our goal, coming in, to take away the big play," linebacker Pepper Johnson said. "Joe got us one time, but mostly he dumped the ball off. It was short stuff all day. We weren't worried about the run; we knew we had to stop Montana. We got after him. I don't care who you are—even the greatest quarterback—you won't be successful with pressure in your face. That was the key to this game—we got to Joe Montana."

Matt Bahr's third field goal made the score 13–9 at the end of the third quarter, setting the stage for an extraordinary, and thrilling, sequence of events.

On a second-down play, 49ers nose tackle Jim Burt—a former Giants sparkplug who had severe back problems and was traded—lunged at Hostetler, whose left leg was planted. Burt's helmet cracked directly on his left knee, and Hostetler was down for several minutes.

Said Lawrence Taylor, "I hollered, 'If that's the way you want to play, that's how we'll play!' But someone else was going to lose a quarterback."

Roll out the Marshall Plan.

The development of Leonard Marshall had been anything but simple. A second-round pick out of LSU in 1983, Marshall had reported to training camp 20 pounds overweight. Team officials assigned a staff spy to make sure he didn't make any late-night fast-food excursions. But Marshall changed. He spent hours in the weight room and evolved into an outstanding partner at inside tackle, playing on the right side of the D-line with Taylor. He had three seasons with double-digit sacks.

With 9:42 left in the game, it was third down at the 49ers' 23, and Montana rolled out. Marshall picked himself up off the ground after

Leonard Marshall separated Joe Montana from the football and ended the quarterback's day to start the Giants' fourth-quarter comeback in the 1991 NFC Championship Game. Photo courtesy of Getty Images

being blocked down, gave chase, and hit Montana squarely between the shoulders from behind. Montana never saw Marshall coming…and never knew what struck him.

"I had to crawl just to get to him, but when I got up, he still had the ball," Marshall said. "It was a good, clean hit, just a football hit, but I knew I hurt him bad. I knew he wasn't going to be back. I could hear him moaning."

It was the third sack of Montana, and not only did the blast knock him woozy and out of the game after completing 18 of 26 passes for 190 yards, he missed the next season and a half with a badly bruised sternum and a fracture of the little finger on his throwing hand.

The 'Niners punted, and another turning-point play was waiting in the wings. It was a daring call by Parcells. On fourth down, linebacker Gary Reasons, the signal-caller on punt formations, took a direct snap in front of punter Sean Landeta and veered right. It was wide open for him, and he lumbered 30 yards to the 16.

"The proverbial gaping hole," Reasons said. "The 49ers were dropping people off the line to set up the return, and I knew I could exploit that." Bahr's fourth field goal, a 38-yarder with 5:47 remaining, cut the lead to one at 13–12, and the gritty Giants, bending but not breaking all season, were in the hunt.

Following the kickoff, Steve Young replaced Montana and promptly completed a 25-yard pass to tight end Brent Jones, but the 49ers went ground-game after that, running the ball on four of Young's five plays, a strategy that proved to be fateful.

With 2:36 left on the ticking clock, Young handed off to Roger Craig on first down for a run up the gut. Nose tackle Erik Howard fought off two blockers and met Craig head-on. The ball popped loose, and LT grabbed it out of the air on the 43. "We weren't surprised that they didn't try to run much throughout the game," Howard said. "But we were surprised they'd try to run in that situation."

In only his seventh career start, Hostetler came through. He rolled out twice and hit Stephen Baker and Mark Bavaro, and all of a sudden, the ball was on the 25.

So with four seconds left, it was up to Bahr, who wasn't even with the club at the start of the season, and who had muffed a 37-yarder wide left earlier in the game. The starting kicker, Raul Allegre, pulled his groin in the third game of the year, and the Giants signed Bahr, who had been axed by the Cleveland Browns in the preseason. To be sure, Bahr had made 17 of 23 field goals during the season, but none was bigger than this, and he had said he'd rather have been a couple touchdowns ahead.

"That's the truth," Bahr revealed, speaking for the lonely kicking fraternity. "In one sense, this kind of situation is what you live and work for as a kicker. But you dread it, too, because so much is on the line. I was nervous, but I felt positive."

Breaking the Ice

Attention, players: be careful what your pals film at parties. They could end up as part of an embarrassing training-camp meeting video. Ask former Giant Brian Mitchell. "We always put together a highlight tape," said head coach Jim Fassel, who wanted to lighten up his team before the first exhibition game one season. "Got hold of a tape of Brian Mitchell about six or seven years ago at a luau, a party, or something.... They had him up there with a bunch of girls in a grass skirt and they had a bow in his hair, and he was doing the hula and everything else in the grass skirt. It was something Delvin Joyce's girlfriend, or fiancée had.... I said, 'Guys, I have highlight tape for the preseason, but some of the new guys I couldn't get enough footage for, so I had to reach back in the archives, and came up with two runs for Brian Mitchell.' He was shocked. The team thought they were going to see a football highlight of him. It was hilarious. They were rolling in the aisles and started high-fiving each other and started teasing him, and at the end of the meeting they were all relaxed and happy, and it was what we needed to do. Mission accomplished. It broke the ice."

Hostetler put the snap down, and Bahr's kick was solid but was starting to tail off toward the left upright. Said snapper DeOssie: "We were all watching it, holding our breath. I'm sure some guys had their eyes closed."

But the kick—an NFC championship–record fifth field goal—stayed straight enough as time expired and lifted the Giants into their second Super Bowl in five years. Hostetler cartwheeled, and a celebration erupted on the Giants sideline.

"Nobody believed we could do this," said Hostetler, whose passing stats (15-for-27 for 176 yards) almost mirrored Montana's. "But there was a strong feeling in this locker room today. We believed in ourselves."

And they played the way they had all season. In eight third-down situations, the 'Niners converted just one. The Giants outgained San Francisco 311 to 240, eliminated the run (only 39 yards on 11 rushes), and controlled the clock, with a 17-minute advantage in time of possession. "It hurts a lot," Craig said. "It was a dream to three-peat, to go all the way. It will take some time to get over this."

The 'Niners walked off the field in stunned disbelief. Lawrence Taylor called it the "greatest game I ever played in because of the stakes and the competitiveness. Everybody expected the 49ers to beat us and three-peat…until Erik jarred the ball loose from Craig and I recovered it to set up Matt's field goal."

"Everyone said we couldn't stop the 49ers," Marshall said. "They deserved all the respect in the world, but no one is invincible. We played physical, aggressive football, and we did it for 60 minutes. We were relentless."

And then he channeled Tony Bennett. "We left our heart here the last time," he said. "But we knew we'd be back to recapture it."

"We weren't the steamrollers we had been the last time," Taylor recalled in a graphic confessional, *LT: Over the Edge*, that detailed his drug use, gambling, and all-night partying in the '80s. "This time we had to fight for everything we got, especially after Phil hurt his foot on December 15 and Jeff Hostetler had to come to our rescue. I didn't think Jeff could win us a championship, but I thought he could win us some games. He surprised me. Third-and-6, third-and-7, he was able to pull that ball down and run for some big first downs. He was able to move the chains. He probably surprised himself."

The launch of Operation Desert Storm in Iraq less than two weeks before the Giants and Buffalo Bills met in Super Bowl XXV cast a shadow of anxiety over Tampa and the hundreds of millions who watched the event. America's minds were elsewhere. There was a legitimate threat of the game being canceled, NFL officials said. Commissioner Paul Tagliabue made the call to play. Security would be immensely tight.

But on the flight from San Francisco to Florida, the team was loose.

Taylor recalled that he was dialing random phone numbers in Tampa and running up and down the aisle yelling, "This is LT. We're coming down there to kick ass!"

On media day, when asked whether he thought the Super Bowl should be played in light of the dire situation in the Persian Gulf, Marshall responded in the affirmative. "It's a struggle for land," he said.

Parcells and defensive coordinator Belichick, the wily generals for the Giants, deployed psychological warfare. "You guys are gonna read a lot of things from my mouth in the press this week," Parcells told the team in a meeting. "Don't believe a word. I'm gonna blow so much smoke up Buffalo's skirts all week. Let 'em start believing how good they are."

The players followed suit in the media, giving the Bills, who had demolished the Raiders 51–3 in the AFC Championship Game, their due. "They're very good," said Mark Collins, the Giants' cornerback. "They're up there with the San Francisco and Washington receivers. Andre Reed is right up there with the best in the sport: very physical, good speed, great hands."

A few days before the game, Parcells showed the Giants a newspaper photo of the Bills being sized for Super Bowl rings. "We got 'em, boys," he beamed.

Taylor recalled Parcells telling him to pick a fight with left tackle Jumbo Elliott in practice, which turned nasty. "It took half the team to separate us," Taylor said. "Nothing personal, though." Later that night Elliott, DeOssie, Erik Howard, and Taylor were out at a club when defensive end Bruce Smith and other Bills took a table about 20 feet away. LT started screaming, "Jumbo's gonna kick your ass, Bruce."

To slow down the Bills' no-huddle offense, Belichick told the defense to "accidentally" kick the ball sometimes after it had been placed on the line of scrimmage. And after plays, "guys would unpile slower than Bill [Parcells] could run the 40," Taylor recalled with a laugh.

The Giants would need every edge possible, because the Bills were for real.

Quarterback Jim Kelly, running back Thurman Thomas, wide receiver Andre Reed, and a top-notch offensive line were the firepower in a go-go offense created by head coach Marv Levy. Like the Giants, they were 13–3 during the season, but came into the game, according to the prophets in Las Vegas, as seven-point favorites.

On game night, January 27, Tampa Stadium was awash in a patriotic sea of hand-held American flags and banners proclaiming "God Bless America" and "Go USA" as the 73,813 fans were determined to show the world a face of unity. Whitney Houston's rendition of the national anthem, a stirring tribute under darkening skies, culminating in a four-jet flyover, never seemed more symbolic, more of a rallying cry.

To counter Kelly's passing attack, the Giants used just two down linemen and spread the remaining nine players to cover and disrupt Reed, the speedy James Lofton, and the other receivers. The Bills went three-and-out on their first possession.

It was Bahr, who sealed the NFC championship win, who pushed the Giants to an early 3–0 lead with a 28-yard field goal after Hostetler led a time-consuming drive of 6:15. The Bills struck back before the end of the quarter, with Lofton gathering in a 61-yard spiral that set the stage for Scott Norwood—who, of course, would later play a major role in this unfolding drama. The Bills kicker nailed a 23-yarder to square the score at 3–3.

Sixteen points were scored in the second quarter, the first nine by Buffalo. Kelly's heroes engineered an 80-yard assault, culminated by a one-yard plunge by little-used backup Don Smith, who had 20 carries all season.

Bruce Smith then tacked on another two points after a Giants miscue deep in their own territory. Running back Ottis Anderson tripped on Hostetler's foot in the backfield, and Smith corralled the quarterback in the end zone for a safety and a 12–3 advantage.

The Giants needed to respond, or the second half would be an uphill climb. Hostetler, however, was far too aware of adversity and having being counted out.

At Penn State, Todd Blackledge beat him out for the starting job, so he transferred to West Virginia. A third-round pick in the 1984 draft, he was relegated to third-string quarterback and emergency tight end. He didn't throw a pass as a pro until 1988.

Media Friendly

Some players like the media, some hate it, some deal with it, and others, well, if they get a chance to join the press corps, use every weapon to get an interview.

Before the 2009 Super Bowl, Giants linebacker Antonio Pierce was on assignment for some media outlet on the jam-packed media day in Tampa, trying to get the attention of some Arizona Cardinals players who were surrounded by cameras and microphones and notebooks. "Excuse me, excuse me!" he shouted while flashing his big ring from the previous Super Bowl win against the Patriots. The ever-resourceful Pierce also gave Cardinals wide receiver Anquan Boldin an air horn and offered some advice. Pierce told him to sound the blaring horn as soon as he heard a reporter ask about his sideline feud with offensive coordinator Todd Haley during the NFC Championship Game. Pierce then asked three questions about Haley. Boldin immediately sounded the horn.

With 3:49 before intermission, the Giants embarked on an impressive, steady, 87-yard march. Hostetler rolled out and found gaps in the secondary. Anderson broke an 18-yarder. Elusive Dave Meggett, primarily a third-down back and peerless kick returner, darted for another 17. Ten plays later, Big Blue was on the Bills 14. But the scoreboard and the down markers on the sideline showed third-and-10. Another three from Bahr would be somehow insufficient.

Instead, a Stephen Baker deke left him in the corner of the end zone, and Hostetler got him the ball for a critical score to close the margin to 12–10.

At halftime, Americans listened to ABC News' Peter Jennings update the situation in Iraq before the football commentators took over to review the game and assess the teams' chances. No one could have predicted the outcome. The Giants allowed an average of just 13 points a game during the season, and the Bills already had put up a dozen.

Some questions were answered on the opening drive: the Giants could still control the ball—and Mark Ingram typified the insistence of this Giants club, the type of never-say-die grit to which DeOssie was referring.

The 9:29 drive that culminated in Anderson's one-yard touchdown to make the score 17–12 involved converting four third-down plays: Hostetler's 11-yard pass to Meggett on third-and-8, a 24-yard run by Anderson on third-and-1, a nine-yard completion to Howard Cross on third-and-4, and one that featured Ingram's determination.

On a third-and-13 at the 32, Hostelter hit Ingram a few yards downfield and many yards short of a critical first down to keep the drive alive. Ingram spun around Kirby Jackson, shook loose from a neck tackle by linebacker Darryl Talley, faked Mark Kelso at the 23, ran right, cut, and as James Williams grabbed his foot, lunged for a final three yards as Talley and two other Bills piled on the slippery receiver at the 18. He had made the first down by a single yard.

"That was the play I remember most," Taylor would recall. "He was four yards short of the first down, but he kicked and he pushed and hopped and got across the marker."

It was Ingram's defining moment as a Giant. He finished the game as the team's top receiver with five catches for 74 yards and later played for the Dolphins and two other teams, but slid into a life of crime afterward.

On the first play of the fourth quarter, a draw from the shotgun, Thomas ran for a 31-yard touchdown, breaking two tackles, and put the Bills back ahead 19–17. Hostetler guided yet another long, 13-play drive that ate up 7:32. Bahr's 21-yard field goal provided the Giants with a slim 20–19 lead.

With just 2:16 to play, Kelly, Thomas, and the Bills made one final thrust, starting from their own 10-yard line. Thomas gained 33 yards on two quality runs, Kelly completed a couple short passes, and with eight seconds left, he spiked the ball at the 29.

Now the spotlight was on Scott Norwood, the team's leading scorer, a former soccer player in northern Virginia who had been accurate throughout his career. In 1990, though, on grass—the surface in Tampa—he was 3-of-7 from beyond 40 yards, and his longest-ever was from 49. This one was right on the edge of his range.

"I wasn't on the field-goal block team at that time in my career," Taylor recalled in his book. But when Norwood lined up, he was there. "I told the guy who usually comes in, 'I ain't leavin'.' You had to be part of the play. It's the worst thing in the world to be sitting on the sidelines, I thought I could block the kick. I thought to myself: *This is like an LT moment.*" It wasn't. Taylor dove and watched from his stomach.

The snap came to holder and backup quarterback Frank Reich, who put the ball down on the right hashmark, the kick started straight then began to drift into infamy. Giants play-by-play announcer Jim Gordon's terse call was: "Snap. Spot. In the air. It's got the distance! It is…no good! Giants win!" But the words that will live in NFL legend were from ABC's Al Michaels: "Wide right!"

No one was more grateful than Hostetler, who had been disparaged by the Bills and other teams. Cornelius Bennett, the linebacker, for example, had said: "If he does decide to run a lot, well, we're not slow. I'm not slow. I've run down a few receivers before. It will be hard for him to get away from us, especially on grass. Besides, we'll prepare for that. A running quarterback is nothing new."

In the jubilant locker room, Hostetler was joyously mocked by teammates. "You can't win. You can't do it. You're just a backup," they roared.

The Bills' room was far more silent. "I knew it was a long kick," said Norwood. "I may have emphasized too much getting my leg into it. It may have affected my follow-through. You don't get a second opportunity. I let a lot of people down."

The Giants, on the other hand, had elevated their game. They choked off the Bills by holding the ball for a Super Bowl record of 40:33. Hostetler had completed 20 of 32 passes for 222 yards and one touchdown. Anderson rushed 21 times for 102 yards and a touchdown and was selected MVP—fulfilling a premonition for the former Miami Hurricane standout.

Anderson, a West Palm Beach native known as "O.J.," recalled how he told a roommate in college, "If I ever played in a Super Bowl and it was in the state of Florida, I would win the MVP Award. I had visions like Joe Namath."

Drafted by the Cardinals in 1979, Anderson did get in a Super Bowl—and scored a late touchdown—while backing up Joe Morris in the Giants' 39–20 rout of Denver in 1987 at the Rose Bowl in Pasadena, not Florida.

After being deemed a short-yardage back nearing the end of his career, he underwent a renaissance in 1989 with the Giants, rushing for 1,023 yards and 14 touchdowns. He was voted Comeback Player of the Year as the Giants won the NFC East. By 1990 the younger Rodney Hampton overtook Anderson, but the rookie from Georgia was hurt midway through the season.

When Norwood lined up, Anderson remembered, "From the angle I had, I couldn't really see…. I looked across the field at the Bills. They were holding hands—and the second the kick went off, they put their hands in the air. And then they dropped them. And that's when I knew the field goal had missed…. It was a dream come true," he said. "And for my family to be close and see me fulfill it [is] an incredible blessing for me. It closed a chapter on my life."

Anderson was one of several Giants videotaped the day before the game by Disney for a tradition that began with Giants quarterback Phil Simms after Super Bowl XXI. The players could say either, "I'm going to Disney World," or, "I dedicate this win to the troops." To his credit, Anderson chose the latter.

Super Bowl XXV was the final game in the New York Giants coaching career of Bill Parcells.

Meanwhile, his counterpart, Thurman Thomas collected an amazing—but largely forgotten—190 yards from scrimmage, rushing 15 times for 135 yards and catching five balls for another 55.

As for Norwood, the following year, during his last NFL season, the much maligned kicker who impressed everyone by standing tall for questions long after others had left in the unhappiest postgame of his life, hit a 44-yarder with 4:18 left in the AFC title game against Denver as the Bills earned a 10–7 win and a Super Bowl berth. The Bills would lose that Super Bowl as well and two more, a heartbreaking sequence that began wide right. The Giants underwent some changes as well.

In Tampa, the 49-year-old Parcells received another Gatorade shower, and Taylor and Carl Banks carried Parcells off the field on their shoulders, a fitting exit for what would be the head coach's final game as a Giant. Four months later, citing health issues, Parcells resigned and was succeeded by offensive coordinator Ray Handley, but would reemerge later in the '90s.

Belichick left to become head coach of the Cleveland Browns, and in February, Tim Mara sold his 50 percent interest in the team to Bob Tisch for a reported $80 million. The sale was actually worked out before the Super Bowl but not announced to avoid distracting the team. For the first time since 1925, the Giants would not be wholly owned by the Mara family.

This number endures: the one-point victory still stands as the narrowest ever in a Super Bowl.

chapter 4

The Four Horsemen,
Trick Plays,
and Sneakers

Conquering the Four Horsemen

If you can't beat 'em, buy 'em...

Imagine combining the New York Mets and the Atlanta Braves. Or the Los Angeles Dodgers and the San Francisco Giants. You'd have an insanely deep team after the merger, right? That's sort of what Tim Mara did.

The Giants' owner—a legal bookmaker who purchased the right to the team in the barnstorming NFL for $500 in 1925—was in trouble. The 1928 season was a 4–7–2 disaster, and no one was attending pro games in the pre-Depression days. College football ruled the roost, and the club couldn't give tickets away.

Mara tried to acquire quarterback Benny Friedman—the league's top passer—from the Detroit Wolverines, who had finished third in 1928, but was snubbed. Undaunted, Mara bought the entire franchise. The brash ploy worked: the rosters were blended, and the Giants marched to a 12–1–1 record in 1929. Ticket sales started to recover. But money couldn't buy everything.

The only loss came to Green Bay that November, 20–6, a win that gave the undefeated Packers the NFL championship. Nonetheless, Mara's edition of the Giants would play a major part in establishing the credibility of the league.

To raise money for New York City's jobless, Mayor Jimmy Walker reached out to Mara and Notre Dame coach Knute Rockne to stage a charity game at the Polo Grounds on the afternoon of December 14, 1930. Rockne declined to bring the current Fighting Irish, who were on their way to another national championship, but offered to assemble a Notre Dame all-star team. A big-name contingent gathered for four days of practice in South Bend, Indiana: the Four Horsemen (quarterback Harry Stuhldreher, halfbacks Jim Crowley and Don Miller, and fullback Elmer Layden), who had not suited up for six years; five of the famous Seven Mules (Adam Walsh, Joe Bach, Rip Miller, Noble Kizer, and Ed Hunsinger); stars of the unbeaten 1929 team such as Jack Cannon, John Law, Tim Moynihan, Ted Twomey, Joe Vezie, John Gebert, and Jack Elder; and Bucky O'Connor and Frank Carideo of the undefeated 1930 team.

The Giants, meanwhile, had fired coach Leroy Andrews and assigned Friedman and tackle Steve Owen to run the team for the game. About 50,000 people showed up for the game, and in his pregame pep talk, Rockne told his players: "Fellows, these Giants are heavy but slow. Go out there, score two or three touchdowns on passes in the first quarter, and then defend."

For Rockne and the Horsemen, the result wasn't exactly pestilence, war, famine, and death, but it was one-sided and embarrassing. Behind the burly line, Friedman ran for two touchdowns and Hap Moran threw one. Rockne's men lost 22–0.

When it was over, Rockne told his team, "That was the greatest football machine I ever saw. I am glad none of you got hurt." The game raised more than $100,000 and was a significant step in establishing the Giants franchise in the Big Apple.

Incidentally, Francis Moran, nicknamed "Hap" for the ever-present smile on his face, was a marvelous player. In 1926 the Iowa native excelled for the Frankford Yellow Jackets and drew this descriptive postgame acclaim from a sportswriter: "Moran was unstoppable, through the line, around the ends, averting the opposing players, and making the longest runs of the game. He seemed like he was right at home, and was different from what went before…like a star let down from the planet Mars with plays that the poor fish of the earth knew nothing about."

Earlier in the 1930 season, against the Packers, Moran took a snap, faked a punt, went around right end, and 91 yards later was tackled from behind by Lavern Dilweg at the 1-yard line. That was the Giants' record for a run from scrimmage for 75 years, until Tiki Barber surpassed it against the Raiders on December 31, 2005.

Moran threw for the final touchdown of the Notre Dame game, which would be the last Rockne coached. He died in a plane crash before the next season.

The First Championship Game

The '30s provided many Decembers to remember for Giants fans.

On December 17, 1933, Wrigley Field in Chicago was cold and misty, but 26,000 hardy souls braved the conditions to witness the first NFL Championship Game. They saw an entertaining contest, replete with trick plays, as the lead changed hands six times.

To assure that no penalties would be called, Giants quarterback Harry Newman told officials prior to the game about deceptive plays his team would employ. It didn't take long. Newman—a former All-American who led the league in passing and set a record with 973 yards gained—called the "Mel Hein Special" in the first quarter, a play that Newman learned, the story goes, in a touch football game from his nieces in Michigan.

Hein was an extremely mobile athlete who played center and nose guard. From a single-wing with an unbalanced line, Newman called a shift, leaving Hein alone at one end of the line as an eligible receiver. Instead of taking the snap from Hein at the 45-yard line, Newman slyly let the center take it back, and turned, fading back to pass. He was flattened by a surprised Bear tackle George Musso, who began looking for the ball.

Hein had put the ball under his jersey and started to saunter downfield. The idea was to wait for blockers. "I got excited and started to run," Hein confessed. He got impatient after 12 yards, and safety Carl Brumbaugh began chasing him and downed him at the 15. The Giants didn't score then, but Newman connected with Red Badgro before the half, and the Giants led 7–6.

No amount of offensive trickery could push the Giants past Bill Hewitt (lateraling) and the Bears in the 1933 NFL Championship Game. Photo courtesy of Getty Images

In the second half, the Bears—moving the ball on runs by Bronko Nagurski—stunned the Giants with a surprise of their own. From the 8, Nagurski headed for the line, suddenly straightened up, and threw a jump pass to right end Bill Karr: touchdown. Bears 16–14, end of the third quarter.

At the other end of the field, on the Bears 8, halfback Ken Strong was trapped near the sideline on a reverse, and improvised a flea-flicker. He lateralled the ball back to Newman, who saw Strong angle across the field and hit him in the end zone. Strong kicked the extra point, and the Giants were ahead 21–16.

As before, the Bears wouldn't play it straight, either. The defense was wary of another jump pass by Nagurski, and at their own 33, were prepared. So when he passed to left end Bill Hewitt, the Giants converged. But Hewitt quickly pitched to Karr, who ran 19 yards for the score. Jack Manders, dubbed "Automatic" for his accuracy, kicked the extra point—he had been 3-for-3 on field goals—and with about two minutes to play, it was 23–21 Bears.

The trickery wasn't over, however.

They set up the Hein Special formation again, and Newman pitched out to Dale Burnett, who was rushed and lofted a weak pass to Hein downfield that was batted away by safety Keith Molesworth. The Bears' Red Grange saved the day, however, diagnosing the last play: a hook-and-lateral.

Newman fired short to Badgro, who was supposed to lateral to Burnett, but when he caught the ball, Grange wrapped up his arms, preventing what could have been a miraculous ending for the Giants.

The Sneakers Game

The first week of December 1934 had been a wet, bone-chilling one in New York City. On Sunday, December 9, the temperature hovered between zero and 10 degrees, and the streets were almost as treacherous as the field uptown at the Polo Grounds.

The NFL championship rematch with the 13–0 Bears had sold out quickly, and 6,000 uncovered, portable seats had been added. The weather scuttled that bonus plan. But the 8–5 Giants had captured some of the city's imagination: winning will do that. Wrapped in quilts, knit caps, snow pants, and other foul-weather gear, 35,059 paying customers showed up in the 20 mph winds.

To be sure, the deck looked stacked against the hometown boys. Newman (broken ribs) and Badgro (broken leg) were out, and the bigger, heavily favored Bears led the league in rushing, passing, and defense.

But the outcome of the game may have been determined that morning after team president Jack Mara visited the icy stadium. The

Bill Parcells, Professor of Football History

If anyone has respect for the game, it is old-school, irascible Bill Parcells. And he believes that many younger players have no sense of the history of the NFL. "I am sure that is true," he said after leaving the Giants. "One time I had a good experience that told me pretty much everything I needed to know. I drafted a young man at New England who turned out to be a really good player named Ty Law. I said I am going to give you No. 24, the same number that Willie Brown wore. And he asked me who Willie Brown was, and Willie Brown is probably the greatest corner to ever play, and that told me all I needed to know. I never forgot it."

tarp was even frozen, he told coach Steve Owen in a phone call. At breakfast, Owen relayed the report to captain Ray Flaherty and tackle Bill Morgan, and Flaherty suggested wearing sneakers for traction rather than cleats. Flaherty's Gonzaga team had worn sneakers on frozen turf against Montana and won. Morgan recalled a similar effect in a college game.

A flurry of phone calls to sporting goods stores went unanswered; they were closed on Sundays. Just before gametime, Owen asked Abe Cohen, a tailor who helped the Giants trainers on weekends and worked for the Manhattan College teams during the week, to borrow some sneakers from the university's locker rooms. Cohen, who had keys to the buildings, left on the mission.

Despite the conditions, Strong kicked a 38-yard field goal. But Nagurski responded, bulling off-tackle for a touchdown, and Manders converted for a 7–3 edge. The Bears continued to move the ball at will, until Morgan stopped a drive and Manders kicked a 17-yarder. The Giants were getting their doors blown off everywhere but on the scoreboard. Another Nagurski TD was nullified by a Hewitt offside, and Manders, who had not missed two field goals in a single game all season, failed on 24- and 38-yarders. Somehow, the Giants survived, down just 10–3 at the half.

As the Giants caught their breath, Cohen hustled through the locker room doors. "Nine pairs was all I could get," he announced. "Didn't have enough time. Hope they do some good."

"I don't know how they decided which players got them," Wellington Mara recalled in 1991, "but I do remember running back

Ken Strong had a pair, and there's a picture of Ed Danowski changing shoes at halftime. So I guess the skill players got them."

According to Barry Gottehrer in *The Giants of New York*, the Giants were late getting back on the field. "What the hell's holding them up?" asked Bears coach George Halas. "They're changing into sneakers," reported reserve guard Walt Kiesling. "Good," snapped Halas, loud enough for the players to hear. "Step on their toes."

Owen emerged with one pair on; Danowski didn't like them at first, but changed his mind after slipping with his cleats on the first drive. With the Bears threatening to score again, Morgan fought his way into the backfield and disrupted three running plays for 34 yards in losses. But on another drive, Manders found his form for a 13–3 lead.

Lineman John Dell Isola and the Giants switched to basketball shoes for the second half of the "Sneakers Game." Photo courtesy of Getty Images

In the fourth quarter, one of the most improbable comebacks in Giants history began. On first down at the Bears 30, Danowski tried a pass to Dale Burnett in the end zone, but the ball was held up in the wind. Carl Brumbaugh jumped in at the 2 and intercepted, but Ike Frankian ripped the ball out of his hands and scored. A Strong conversion trimmed the margin to three.

Observing from the press box, Columbia University coach Lou Little thought Owen should take more advantage of the sneakers. He suggested a cut-back play, with Strong faking a run to his left to lure the defense, then knifing off-tackle to the right. The blocking was perfect, Strong got through the line, bounced off an official, and ran past the Bears' sliding secondary for a 42-yard score.

The sneakers were providing a grip. Strong used a reverse to cap another drive from the 11. The Giants led 23–13, and after an interception, Danowski found his way in from the 9. Scoring 27 points in the last 15 minutes had given the Giants a 30–13 win.

"I think the sneakers gave them the edge in the second half," said Nagurski. "They were able to cut back when they were running with the ball, and we weren't able to cut with them."

Inside the delirious locker room, the Giants celebrated their good fortune, which included a $621 check for each frostbitten player. Danowski completed 6 of 11 passes for 83 yards; Morgan had won some more admirers; and Strong's 17 points would remain an NFL Championship Game record for almost 30 years.

The Rest of the Roaring '30s

The Giants were 9–3 in 1935 but were soundly beaten 26–7 by the Lions in the championship game. They missed the playoffs in 1936 and 1937, but the following year provided another campaign for the scrapbook.

For the fourth time in six years, the Giants represented the Eastern Conference in the title game. They had beaten the Green Bay Packers three weeks previously, and on December 11, hoped to show that game was not a fluke and win a second championship.

The Guarantee

With the Giants at 7–4 and having lost two straight in 2000, head coach Jim Fassel was tired of the questions about his club. So he made a brash vow. On the day before Thanksgiving, Fassel declared, "I'm shoving my chips to the center of the table. I'm raising the ante. This team is going to the playoffs."

Fassel should have been in Vegas. The Giants won five straight to finish 12–4 and beat the Eagles in the first playoff round. Then, Kerry Collins, a recovering alcoholic who was signed to a $16 million contract in 1999, threw for 381 yards and five touchdowns in the 41–0 vanquishing of the Vikings in the conference championship game.

Even co-owner Wellington Mara was giddy. "This is the Giants team that was referred to as the worst ever to win homefield advantage in the NFL," he said. "Today, on this field of painted mud, we proved that we're the worst team to ever win the National Football League conference championship."

Unfortunately, Fassel didn't have another guarantee in him.

Two weeks later, Collins was 15-for-39 and fired four interceptions in the 34–7 loss to the Ravens in Super Bowl XXXV.

This was a war of attrition. Green Bay's Don Hutson injured a knee; Hein had a concussion; other players left the field battered as well. Defense reigned early. Defensive end Jim Lee Howell, who later would coach the team, blocked Clarke Hinkle's punt, and Ward Cuff's 14-yard field goal provided a 3–0 boost. Jim Poole, the other end, blocked a punt by Cecil Isbell, and Tuffy Leeman's six-yard scamper put the Giants ahead 9–0.

The teams traded scores, as Danowski, the Fordham grad who was a driving force in the Sneakers Game four years earlier, threw an interception but recouped with a 21-yard TD pass to Hap Barnard. The Giants clung to a 16–14 halftime lead. A field goal in the third lifted the Packers to a one-point lead, 17–16.

For the rest of the game, two players, Danowski and Hank Soar, would leave their mark on the Roaring '30s for the Giants. Soar was raised in Pawtucket, Rhode Island, and attended Providence College, but left after his junior year for the Boston Shamrocks of the AFL. The Giants signed him in 1937, and he played until 1946. From 1950 to 1975, he was one of baseball's top umpires, and worked first base at Don

Larsen's perfect game in the 1956 World Series. In his nine years with the Giants, Soar—who played through 17 fractures—played defensive back, runner, and receiver, but caught just two touchdowns in the regular season, which is why this game was so unusual. He was ruggedly capable, but hardly a star.

With fourth-and-1 on the Green Bay 44, and the Giants down 17–16, Danowski checked Owen's signal on the sideline. "I gave him the sign to buck," said Owen. "I knew that's what he wanted to call. He did. Soar made the first down." The drive was alive.

Five plays later, from the 23, Soar and Poole were lined up side-by-side on the outside and ran straight downfield. A crowd gathered at the 7, where Danowski aimed. Poole, Hinkle, and Herm Schneidman leaped.

"It was just a jump ball, and I out-jumped a bunch of guys from Green Bay," said Soar. Hinkle tried to tackle Soar at the 3, but he plowed over the goal line. It would be the title-clinching touchdown. The Giants then led 23–17, but barely held on. Near the end of the game, Giants defensive backs batted down three consecutive passes in the end zone.

In the dressing room, the limping Giants sprayed beer and lifted Owen onto their shoulders. For Danowski, known as "Easy Ed," it was his second championship. But he was overshadowed by the exploits of

Fair-Weather Fans

The media notices. Players notice. But Jim Fassel, like many coaches, doesn't care if fans desert the stadium before the game is over. Especially early in a season.

"There is no question that when you are a player or you're a coach, you are not going to quit, we are just starting this fight," he said. "Everyone is going to say what is wrong with this team, just like after the first week of the season, most of the teams that lost that first week, people said they were no good, get them out of the picture. That is not when you are in the arena. When you are in there doing the fighting, that is not your attitude, that shouldn't be your attitude. So if a player like Jeremy Shockey feels like, 'Hey, stay in your seat until this thing is over, we are going to keep fighting,' that is a pretty natural reaction. A fan sitting up there with six minutes to go and they just scored, it's a 13-point lead, hey, I want to beat the traffic out of here. So you have two different outlooks. I don't care, I am playing a game."

quarterbacks such as Friedman, Charlie Conerly, Y.A. Tittle, and others in the modern era.

In the single-wing, the halfback was the primary passer, and Danowski was the NFL's leading passer in 1935 and in 1938, when he was 70-of-129 for 848 yards and seven touchdowns. He also led the Giants all four years. Danowski, who grew up in Riverhead, Long Island, starred at Fordham until joining the Giants in 1934 and later coached the Rams from 1946 to 1955.

The Giants would have one last hurrah—albeit a controversial one—at the Polo Grounds, on December 3, 1939, when they beat the Redskins 9–7 for the Eastern Conference title. About 12,000 of the 62,000-plus at the game were Redskins fans who made the trek north.

Ward Cuff, a former roommate and longtime friend of Wellington Mara, kicked two field goals and Ken Strong one for all the Giants scoring, and Bob Masterson caught a 20-yard pass for the Redskins in the fourth quarter.

In the closing seconds, Washington's Bo Russell tried a 15-yard field goal, but referee Bill Halloran ruled it went over one upright, not between the two. Coach Ray Flaherty went ballistic. "It was plenty inside. Every cop in back of the goalposts said so," he said. "If Halloran has a conscience, he'd never again sleep an untroubled night." When the clock ran out, players and fans stormed the field. Halloran had to be escorted by police after the Redskins' Ed Justice tried to punch him.

So the decade, which began with a worthy charity game, ended with a riot.

The Frustrating '40s

In the 1940s the Giants would reach the championship game three times in the first seven seasons—years that were interrupted by the war—but would never win, losing twice to the Bears and once to the Packers.

Two games symbolized the Giants' ineptness. Both were November 1943.

The Lions and Giants played a scoreless tie in a cold, steady rain in Briggs Stadium. Neither offense went past the opponents' 15. There hasn't been a scoreless tie in the NFL since.

The following week, Chicago quarterback Sid Luckman threw seven touchdowns against the Giants in a 56–7 demolition, a record that would stand alone for 12 years.

By 1946 Mara had given over complete control of the team to his two sons. Jack controlled the business, while Wellington oversaw the on-field operations. They struggled from 1947 to 1949, never finishing above .500.

chapter 5

Giants in Their Day

Speed to Burn:
Homer Jones and Choo-Choo Roberts

Homer Carroll Jones was a Texan who could run the 100-yard-dash in
9.3 seconds. Gene "Choo-Choo" Roberts was no slouch either. At the
University of Tennessee–Chattanooga, Roberts ran the 100 in 9.8. Such
speed was rare for the Giants, and these two burners were record-setters
in different decades. And both their Giants careers were short—but
swift.

Jones was an unusual physical specimen. At 6'2" and 220 pounds,
he starred in track and field and football at Texas Southern College (now
Texas Southern University). In 1963 the 22-year-old was drafted in the
fifth round by the Houston Oilers of the American Football League, but
suffered a knee injury in training camp and was cut.

The Giants, who had drafted him in the 20ᵗʰ round, offered Jones
a bus ticket to New York and to pay for his knee surgery. The operation
didn't slow Jones down a bit. Homer was still the master of the long ball.
Quarterback Fran Tarkenton said flinging the ball downfield to Jones
was like "throwing to a man riding a motorcycle holding a butterfly net."

On October 17, 1965, at Yankee Stadium, not only did Jones
display his blazing speed, he may have started a trend. In a 35–27 defeat
of the Eagles. Jones beat Irv Cross down the left sideline for 89 yards and
fired the ball to the turf behind him, a move that he called the "spike,"
after crossing the goal line.

Jones had seen Frank Gifford and the Packers' Paul Hornung flip the
ball to fans in the stands after scoring, but he opted for his personal

stamp, one that has since evolved—for better or worse—into much more elaborate celebrations.

The following season, he caught the longest pass in Giants history, 98 yards from Earl Morrall. "I'd never been able to overthrow him in practice," Morrall said. "I figured I hang one up there. As it was, he had to wait for the ball."

In 1967 Jones had his best season statistically, catching 49 passes for 1,209 yards, an average of 24.7 yards, and 13 touchdowns, which led the NFL. He was third in the league in combined rushing and receiving yards from scrimmage behind the Browns' Leroy Kelly and the Cardinals' Jackie Smith, and made the Pro Bowl that season and the next.

At the 1967 Pro Bowl in Los Angeles, one of the gimmicks proposed was a 100-yard-dash between Jones and Dallas Cowboys ex-track star Bob Hayes to determine who was the fastest. It never came off because the Giants asked Jones to pull out, and Homer was often asked who would have won. His answer was: "What hurts more, getting hit by a .22-caliber bullet [referring to Hayes' number and his smaller stature, 5'11", 185 pounds] or a .45-caliber bullet [Jones' number and larger frame]?"

In January 1970 Jones was traded to the Browns for running back Ron Johnson and veteran defensive lineman Jim Kanicki. Knee injuries finally brought Homer to earth, and he retired at age 29 in 1971.

Jones concluded his career with 224 receptions for 36 touchdowns and 4,986 yards, an average of 22.3 yards per catch, still an NFL record for players with a minimum of 200 career receptions. No Giants receiver has been to the Pro Bowl since Jones went in 1968. About one of every six of his receptions resulted in a TD.

• • •

Gene Roberts chugged into town first, but is the far lesser-known talent.

Born in 1923, Roberts attended high school in Kansas City, Missouri, made his Giants debut in 1947, and played with them until 1950. "Choo-Choo," of course, came from the popular song with Chattanooga in the title, and he rolled onto the tracks in New York quickly. Against the Bears on October 23, 1949, Roberts caught four

Not Just a Short-Yardage Back

Brandon Jacobs didn't want to be a linebacker, a guard, or a defensive end, he told his coaches at Auburn and Southern Illinois. And the 6'4", 260-pound Giants running back who runs the 40-yard dash in 4.6, dislikes it even more when critics tried to pigeonhole him as a short-yardage specialist. But Jacobs doesn't dance and deke behind the line of scrimmage. "There is most definitely more to my game; as far as just being a short-yardage back, I'm going to surprise a lot of people when they only ask for one yard and I take it the distance," Jacobs said. "I don't pitter-patter behind the line of scrimmage. I know the down and distance. I know where I have to go, so I get the rock and I barrel down and I just get in. Just one person won't stop me from getting what I want. It's going to be a couple people."

passes from Charlie Conerly, three of them for touchdowns of 85, 62, and 29 yards and a 201-yard day.

With his running and receiving skills, Roberts was the prototype for Frank Gifford and Tiki Barber. In 1949 he scored a league-high 17 touchdowns: nine on the ground to go with 634 rushing yards, and eight through the air to go with 35 receptions for 711 yards. He was the first back to have two games of 200 receiving yards.

Then, on November 12, 1950, against the Chicago Cardinals, Roberts set the NFL and Giants single-game rushing record with 218 yards. The NFL record stood for six years before it was broken by Tommy Wilson of the Los Angeles Rams on December 16, 1956. The Giants' mark lasted far longer, into the next millennium, 55 years. Barber broke it on December 17, 2005.

Once he started running, few could catch Roberts. One who could was Bill Willis, a nose guard who was signed by Paul Brown for Cleveland's team in the All-American Football Conference in 1946, before Jackie Robinson broke baseball's color barrier. Willis, a Hall of Famer, had a splendid career. But his most distinctive play may have been when he chased down Roberts from behind after a long run at the 4-yard line, saving a touchdown and preserving the Browns' 8–3 playoff victory on December 17, 1950. The Browns defeated the Los Angeles Rams the following week for their first NFL title. Said Dante Lavelli, who played with Willis at both Ohio State and in Cleveland, "That was his most outstanding play."

Choo-Choo was even difficult to derail north of the border.

Charlie Conerly spent his entire 14-year career with the Giants. Photo courtesy of Getty Images

When Roberts left the Giants in 1950, he began playing for the Ottawa Rough Riders of the Canadian Football League. In 1953 he led the CFL in scoring with 88 points, making him the only player ever to lead both leagues in scoring.

Charlie Conerly: Good Time Charlie and Big Blue

The Mississippi state slogan is *Virtute et Armis* ("By Valor and Arms").

The Giants were fortunate to have two of the strongest arms that Ole Miss produced: Eli Manning and Charlie Conerly. Long before Eli, whose father and brother were NFL household names, there was Charlie Conerly, a poor kid from a Clarksdale household. Although Conerly enrolled at the University of Mississippi in 1941, he served three years as a Marine at Iwo Jima and in Guam before returning to Ole Miss to set NCAA records as a single-wing tailback for the Rebels. Among them: most passing yards (1,367), pass completions (133), and consecutive passes without an interception (61), all in 1947. Those records remained until 1969, when they were broken by Archie Manning, Eli's dad.

Conerly's career is memorialized by the Conerly Trophy, given annually to the best college football player in the state.

In 1945, while in the service, the Redskins selected him in the 13th round of the draft. But by 1947, Washington was set at quarterback with Sammy Baugh and traded Conerly to the Giants in 1948. By that time, Conerly's hair was prematurely silver at 27, and his lined face made him seem much older. He had worn No. 42 in high school and college, and because this was before the NFL rules on numbering players by position, he was allowed to retain it as a quarterback. Conerly's number would be retired by the team in 1962, a year after he retired at age 40.

In his first season in offensive coach Allie Sherman's T formation, Conerly was named Rookie of the Year after throwing for 2,175 yards and 22 touchdowns, the latter an NFL record for a rookie. That record was in turn broken in 1998 by another Manning: Peyton, of the Indianapolis Colts.

Two years later, Conerly and the Giants became the first NFL team to ever play outside of the U.S., when they met the Ottawa Rough Riders in a preseason exhibition game at Lansdowne Park, Ottawa, on

August 12. Before 15,000 fans, the Giants won 27–6. It was an unusual matchup, to say the least. The first half was played under Canadian rules and scoring; the second half, according to U.S. rules.

Despite only three downs, the Giants led 13–6, with Tom Landry—who would later be an assistant coach with the Giants and legendary head coach of the Dallas Cowboys—as punter and quarterback. Ottawa scored in the first two minutes on a pass, which gave them five points, and the conversion failed. According to the *New York Times* story on the game, one of the few accounts available, Landry punted into the end zone for a point—a Canadian "rouge." Landry's passes moved the ball downfield for a Steve Hatfield seven-yard run and a Ray Poole extra point that made the score 7–5. Another Ottawa rouge made it 7–6. A 60-yard run was called back when Giants end Al Schmidt was downfield blocking—a no-no beyond 10 yards of scrimmage. The Giants also received a 15-yard penalty for high tackling but led 13–6 at the half when Hatfield scored again. In the second half, Conerly came in and was 8-for-10 passing on drives that ended with halfback Bob Griffith scoring on one and two-yard plunges. Oh, Canada!

Back in the states, because the Giants had a less-than-formidable offensive line in his first few years, Conerly—hailed for his toughness—

Q&A with Coach Coughlin

In coaching, it's all theoretical sometimes. Follow this comical exchange between a writer and Tom Coughlin when the coach was asked about the status of wide receiver James McKnight.

Q: Is James McKnight still on this team?

A: In theory, yes.

Q: In theory?

A: Yes.

Q: How about in reality?

A: He's not out here. He's not practicing. That's to be determined.

Q: What happened?

A: He had the injury and he's had some further information, so he can't practice.

Q: He's here at camp?

A: He's not physically here. He's still physically on our team. But that has to be decided.

took a beating. In 1952 or 1953 his friend and roommate, the great back Frank Gifford, recalled that Conerly played the entire season with a shoulder separation.

In one game against the Eagles on October 26, 1952, in Philadelphia, he was hammered by defensive end Norm "Wild Man" Willey. In Philadelphia's 14–10 win, Willey had double-digit sacks, some say 15 to 17, most of Conerly, although records are sketchy.

After a particularly bad day against Cleveland, according to Gifford, Conerly—among the more laid-back and affable of the Giants—struggled to his feet and hobbled to the huddle. "Would any of you guys," he asked, "like to come back here and throw this thing?"

After the 1953 season, when the Giants went 3–9, he was booed when introduced during a New York Rangers game at Madison Square Garden, and fans ridiculed him with jeers and banners reading "Goodbye, Charlie" at games, Conerly wanted to retire and returned to his cotton farm.

Coach Jim Lee Howell, the new Giants coach, paid him a visit, vowed that the blocking would improve, and convinced Conerly, 33, to give New York another shot. With more quality players, the Giants would march to the NFL championship in 1956. Now 35, Conerly— mentored by offensive genius Vince Lombardi—was even more effective. He had his own table at Toots Shor's, and his wife Perian (pronounced Perry-Anne) was writing columns about the team as a freelancer for the *Times*. And the rugged Conerly would appear in an ad campaign as the "Marlboro Man." Life was better.

Cleveland Browns coach Paul Brown said that Conerly was one of the toughest quarterbacks to "red-dog," the name for blitz at the time, because of his quick release. Along with Gifford and Kyle Rote, he engineered a 47–7 pasting of the Chicago Bears in the title game in their first year at Yankee Stadium. "I got most of the accolades that year," Gifford said, "but we knew who got us there."

In 1958 Conerly almost got the Giants there again. He relieved starter Don Heinrich early—a common strategy in Lombardi's two-quarterback system—in the championship game against the Baltimore Colts. In the fourth quarter, he directed two drives to provide a 17–14 lead before the Colts tied the "Greatest Game Ever Played" and won it on Alan Ameche's TD in sudden-death overtime. Conerly was initially voted the MVP before the comeback, when a revote put Unitas on top.

The Giants also won the Eastern Conference and lost to the Colts in 1959. Conerly was named league MVP.

Here's a remarkable stat: only 42 quarterbacks all-time have had season ratings over 100. In 1959 Conerly produced a 102.7 quarterback rating, higher than Unitas. He threw just four interceptions in 194 attempts.

No passer cracked 100 in the 11 years before 1959. Before that, Sid Luckman and Sammy Baugh headed the small list. Y.A. Tittle, who would replace Conerly, would post a rating of 104.8 in 1963, but Conerly held most of the Giants' career passing records until Phil Simms broke them about a quarter-century later.

As a backup for Tittle, Conerly guided many a comeback, but his career was winding down. "If you win, you're an old pro; if you lose, you're an old man," he said. The Mississippi Delta beckoned.

And, appropriately, on Charlie Conerly Day at the Stadium, November 29, 1959, he was presented with cotton seed, a trailer, and a hefty amount of fertilizer.

His teammates used another term for fertilizer when Conerly, who died in 1996, was bypassed for the Hall of Fame. He is among only a few quarterbacks who have won league championships—and MVP awards—and are not enshrined. "When I got in," said Gifford, "I was embarrassed to be there when Charlie wasn't."

Ray Flaherty: Innovator, Motivator

The story goes that when quarterback Sammy Baugh was taking the field for his first practice session with the Washington Redskins in 1937, head coach Ray Flaherty handed him the football.

"They tell me you're quite a passer," Flaherty reportedly said.

"I reckon I can throw a little," Baugh replied.

"Show me," Flaherty said, pointing down the field. "Hit that receiver in the eye."

To which Baugh supposedly responded, "Which eye?"

Atta Boy

It's not always game balls that are awarded after games. Coach Jim Fassel had "Atta Boys." After beating the 6–0 Vikings in 2003, guard Ian Allen—who had been previously benched—was one recipient.

"I told him this in front of the whole team when I was handing out game balls and 'Atta Boys,'" Fassel said. "I said, 'Ian, I had to bench you, okay? And I had to play you again, I needed you again. You need to work on your technique, you need to work on some assignments, you need some work to hone in on your skills and become a better player, but I will live with that.' Because what I saw in him yesterday, that I hadn't seen in him before and I was very proud of him—he had fight. He fought, he finished every play; he was battling. As long as he will give me that kind of toughness and effort; he will finish plays all the way then, we will keep living with it. That is why he got an 'Atta Boy,' because he played well."

More "Atta Boys" were not on the radar for Allen. He later played a year for the Eagles and another for Arizona. But he is now in the ownership ranks. He works for Sky Sports NFL TV programming in the UK and in March 2008 purchased the Ipswich Cardinals British American Football Club.

Keeping an eye on things—and his mind on football—was certainly a winning trait of Flaherty's, from his years in the American Football League to eight years with the Giants to his successful tenure as coach of the Redskins.

In the 1934 NFL Championship Game, played on the skating rink that the Polo Grounds became in the icy weather, it was Flaherty—the team captain—who echoed a suggestion that the Giants try sneakers for traction, a tactic that worked when he was a star at Gonzaga University in Washington in the mid-1920s.

The newly shod Giants, having secured nine pairs from Manhattan College, came back from a halftime deficit to rumble past the Bears 30–13. On the other hand, some downplayed the sneakers' effect. A couple players believed that, had the Bears simply replaced the worn-down nubs on their cleats, Chicago might have won.

A two-way end in the golden era of rushing, the red-haired, freckle-faced Flaherty had led the NFL in receptions and yardage, with 21 catches for 350 yards, in 1932. Born in Spokane, Flaherty has the distinction of being the first pro football player ever to have his number retired. The Giants decommissioned his No. 1 in 1935, after eight years with the team.

After the 1935 season, when the Giants lost 26–7 in Detroit to the Lions in the title game, Boston Redskins owner George Preston Marshall came calling. He signed Flaherty as head coach after a 2–8–1 season, and Flaherty, who was earning about $400, made a brash statement: he offered to retire if the team didn't win the title.

On hearing of the signing of Wayne Millner, Flaherty wired Marshall: "With that big Yankee playing end, please accept my resignation if we do not win the championship this year!"

The 1936 team won the Eastern Division, but nothing else. Marshall didn't care. He was concerned about poor attendance in Boston. In 1937 Marshall moved the franchise to Washington. Flaherty stayed for six more years. In all, he led the team to two NFL championships and four divisional titles. His winning percentage of .735 (47–16–3) is the best among Washington coaches.

When the Redskins won the title in 1937, Flaherty introduced the behind-scrimmage screen pass—now a staple of the pro and college attack—as a way to avoid the Bears' ferocious rush on Baugh, the rookie. "They were breaking their necks trying to rack up Baugh," Flaherty recalled. "That's what made the screen pass go. It had been nullified downfield, but we put it behind the line and the Bears didn't know how to stop it." Baugh threw three touchdown passes in the 28–21 win.

In 1940 Flaherty absorbed the worst defeat in NFL history, a 73–0 drubbing by the Bears in the title game. Two years later the Redskins won the East with an impressive 10–1 record, and before the title tilt against the Bears, Flaherty wrote the score up on the blackboard before the game and addressed the team, a 20-point underdog.

"Flaherty told us he didn't care whether we won the game or not but just to beat the living s— out of them," recalled guard Clyde Shugart in the *Redskins Encyclopedia*. "He got kind of choked up, and [assistant coach] Turk Edwards started to say something and the same thing happened. I always said that if somebody hadn't opened the door, we would have run right through it to get out on the field."

In that game, Flaherty used a two-platoon offense, a passing-oriented one with Baugh and a specialized running unit with tailback Frank Filchock. "We made the defenses change," he told Don Smith, writing for the *Coffin Corner*. "They'd get all set for Baugh's passing and would have to change when we put the running unit in. We kept them constantly off balance and usually succeeded." The Skins scored twice to win 13–7.

As the final seconds ticked off, 36,000 fans at Griffith Stadium rushed the field, pulled down the goal posts, ripped up the turf, and fought their way in the locker room.

After a year in the Navy in 1945, Flaherty coached the All-America Football Conference's New York Yankees and won division titles in each of his two full seasons there. He spent 1949 as coach of the AAFC Chicago Hornets.

Flaherty was inducted into the Pro Football Hall of Fame in 1976 for his contributions as a coach. For his career, Flaherty won 80 games, lost 37, and managed five ties, for a .684 lifetime winning percentage. He died on July 19, 1994, at age 89.

"He was an excellent coach, a hard-driving coach," said Shugart. "He kept everybody on the ball and under control. He wasn't soft. He kept our noses to the grindstone."

Even Baugh had words of tribute: "He did a hell of a job. He was a good man, a good football man. Our boys had a lot of hope when Flaherty was there."

Benny Friedman: The Jewish Johnny U

In the 1920s football was indicative of its name. The melon-shaped ball was carried by rushers and kicked. It was difficult to grip, and in fact, the rules discouraged throwing the ball forward. A passer had to stand at least five yards behind the line of scrimmage, two consecutive incompletions triggered a penalty, and an incomplete pass in the end zone turned the ball over to the opponent. Roughing the passer? Hah. It was anything goes.

Enter Benny Friedman, a 5'8", 170-pounder from Cleveland, born to Orthodox immigrants from Russia. He turned out to be a real

game-changer, a player who would be credited with not only revolution-
izing the tactics of the game of football, but the ball itself.

In high school, Friedman was an old-school gym rat, lifting weights
and gripping and squeezing a tennis ball or handball to strengthen his
wrist and fingers. He spread and stretched his hands on railings and arm-
rests, the story goes, and before he finished his freshman year at the
University of Michigan, he said, "I was able to wrap my hand around a
football and grip it as firmly as a pitcher grips a baseball." The baseball
analogy goes a step further. Friedman would be one of the first quarterbacks to step into the pocket, and he never threw sidearm or three-
quarters. He brought his arm up directly over his head, cocked the ball,
and threw down, with his feet, head, and arm aligned with the intended
receiver. And his follow-through also resembled a pitcher's, with his arm
coming down low to the ground.

In 1925 and 1926, the Wolverines soared to 7–1 seasons and first
place in the Big Ten. Against Indiana in 1925, Friedman threw five
touchdowns and kicked two field goals and eight extra points. "In Benny
Friedman, I have one of the greatest passers and smartest quarterbacks in
history," said Michigan coach Fielding Yost. "He never makes a mistake,
and as for football brains, it's like having a coach on the field when
Benny is out there calling signals."

A two-time All-American, Friedman intended to study law, but
decided to turn pro to earn money to assist his ailing father. So Friedman
signed with the NFL's Cleveland Bulldogs, and when the Bulldogs folded
after the 1927 season, Friedman signed with the Detroit Wolverines.

With his running ability and willingness to pass on any down,
Friedman led the NFL in touchdown passes in 1927 and in 1928 led the
NFL in that category, rushing touchdowns, scoring, and extra points.
"Why wait until third down when the defense is looking for it?" he
declared in his 1931 biography, *The Passing Game*.

At that time in the fledgling NFL, the Giants were struggling, both
on the field and at the box office. The Wolverines would not part with
Friedman, so Giants owner Tim Mara boldly bought the entire franchise
and paid Friedman $10,000 a year. Most players earned about $1,000.
The money was well spent. With the Giants in 1929, Friedman—who
wore No. 1—led the league again with 20 touchdown passes. At the Polo

Grounds on November 17, 1929, he threw four touchdown passes against the Bears in a 34–0 rout.

No NFL team would surpass 20 passing touchdowns in a season until 1942. And 1942 would be 10 years after the league removed all of its restrictions against passing—and slimmed down the ball's size and shape to make passing easier and more accurate. Friedman did it the old-fashioned way, and he had a touch.

"When a Friedman pass reaches the receiver, it has gone its route," sportswriter Paul Gallico wrote. "The ball is practically dead. The receiver has merely to reach up and take hold of it like picking a grapefruit off a tree. That is Benny's secret, and that is why so many of his passes are completed. He is the greatest forward passer in the history of the game."

Friedman played just six years in the NFL in an era when stats were disparately compiled. But working from newspaper accounts, sportswriters figured that Friedman passed for at least 5,653 yards (50 percent more than the closest competitors) and 55 touchdowns, more than double that of any others.

"I think the most amazing thing about him was the way he could throw the kind of football that was in use in his days," said Giants' co-owner Wellington Mara. "Did you ever see that ball? It was like trying to throw a wet sock."

With the Giants a success, the NFL was on more solid footing.

In 1931 Friedman asked Mara if he could buy a piece of the team, but Mara declined, saying he wanted to keep the club in the family's hands. So Friedman accepted the offer of Bill Dwyer, owner of the Brooklyn football Dodgers, to quarterback and coach in 1932. After two seasons, Mayor Fiorello LaGuardia asked Friedman to coach the City College of New York's team. "I didn't know pro football was going to progress as much as it did," Friedman said. "If I had, I might have stayed in."

After Friedman retired, so did the memories of his career. In fact, he wound up at odds with the league in a court battle to include pre-1958 players in the pension benefits plan. He finally was inducted, far too late, posthumously, into the Hall of Fame in 2005.

Friedman lost his leg to diabetes at the age of 72. He committed suicide four years later.

Hinkey Haines:
A Yankee, Then the First Giants Star

Even before he joined the Giants, running back Henry Luther Haines had basked in the glow of New York sports success. Well, at least he was warmed by the glow.

On April 20, 1923, Haines made his major league baseball debut with the New York Yankees at the age of 24. The speedy little right-handed outfielder from Lebanon Valley College and Penn State played in just 28 games that season, the year Yankee Stadium opened, mostly as a pinch runner and defensive replacement on a team of stars such as Babe Ruth, Lou Gehrig, Waite Hoyt, and Bob Meusel. Haines had modest numbers: four hits, two of them doubles, nine runs scored, three RBIs, and three stolen bases. The Yankees went 98–54, and he appeared in two World Series games against the New York Giants, going 0-for-1 but scoring a run.

For Haines, nicknamed "Hinkey" by his former boarding-school mates, the best was yet to come. He signed on with the Giants in 1925—the club's first NFL season—and, although 26, became their finest player and main attraction in the late '20s, when the NFL was light years away from the multibillion-dollar business it is today. Not only was Haines a key Giant, he also would become the only athlete to ever win championships in both the NFL and major league baseball.

In 1925 the Giants dropped their first three games. But on November 1, they got a glimpse of the breakaway speed that Hinkey displayed at Penn State on October 30, 1920, when he broke loose for two 90-yard touchdown runs against archrival Penn in a 28–7 victory.

The Giants cracked the win column for the first time that week. In a 19–0 defeat of Cleveland, Haines scored twice, on a run and a pass reception, and the Giants won the rest of their regular-season games.

Against Providence, a week after a bloody contest with the Columbus Tigers in which players were carried off and Haines had his nose broken, he saved the game in the final minutes with the Giants ahead 13–10. On fourth down at his own 5, Hinkey, wearing a leather mask to protect his nose, dropped back into punt formation and touched the ball down in the end zone for a safety. The G-men held on for a one-point win.

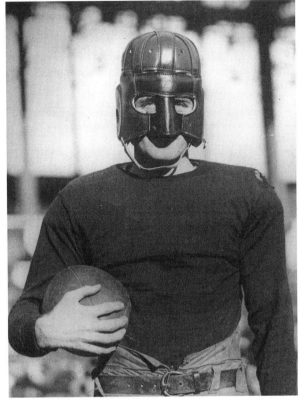

Hinkey Haines, shown here wearing a leather mask to protect his broken nose, was the first athlete to play for championship teams in both major league baseball and the NFL. Photo courtesy of Getty Images

The team's marketing department jumped aboard. Ads read: "Come see Hinkey Haines and his New York Football Giants." The Giants, who'd had to give tickets away, actually began selling them.

In 1926 Haines was involved in two touchdowns in a game against Providence. Against the Cardinals, he scored twice, on a twisting 80-yard run and a 20-yard pass. The next season against Red Grange and the Bears, Haines showed his savvy. Steve Owen, who called the game "the roughest, toughest I ever played in," described Haines' game-turning move in a publication called the *Coffin Corner*:

> Haines called one of the smartest plays I ever seen to win for us. He stage-managed it perfectly. The Bears had plodded downfield to our 1-yard line, where we held 'em. Haines signaled for punt formation. The Bears dropped two men back to midfield and

jammed nine on the line. We called signals in the open in those days and Haines yelled to Mule Wilson, our punter, to be careful not to step beyond the end line for a safety. He asked that a towel be brought out to wipe the ball because there was a patch of mud here and there on the field. Haines completely fooled the Bears. When the ball was snapped he had dropped back a few yards to receive it. He threw over the line to Chuck Corgan [an end], and Chuck went to the Bears' 40-yard line.

The Giants held on to win 13–7 and finished 11–1–1 to claim the championship.

Combine that gridiron intelligence with blazing speed, and it didn't matter that Haines was just 5′10″, 168 pounds. Haines twice was named college All-America in baseball and lettered in basketball, and probably could have lettered in track, but football coach Hugo Bezdek would not let him formally enter any events, although Haines had beaten everybody on the track team in sprints. Ralph Davis, a sports columnist of the day, wrote, "Haines is the logical collegiate successor of the famous Jim Thorpe...he is certainly the Thorpe of the present day." And Bob Folwell, the Giants' first coach, contended that in 20 years of coaching, he had never seen a faster man on the field.

As recounted in Barry Gottehrer's *The Giants of New York*, in 1926 a sportswriter penned a poem celebrating the running back in the newspaper, and teammates pasted it to the locker room wall:

> *Oh Hinkey Haines, oh Hinkey Haines!*
> *The New York Giants' football brains*
> *He never loses, always gains*
> *Oh Hinkey Haines, oh Hinkey Haines!*

Haines' career, which started with a bang, ended with a whimper. He wanted to retire before the 1928 season, but owner Tim Mara talked him into another season. The Giants finished sixth, and Hinkey was sidelined by a neck injury. He finished his career with the Staten Island Stapletons in 1931.

Kyle Rote: From Triple Threat to Renaissance Man

It is an eerie parallel.

Two knee injuries a few months apart in 1951 damaged the careers of two famous New York athletes.

On October 5, in the fifth inning of Game 2 of the World Series, Giants star Willie Mays lofted a short fly ball to the outfield at Yankee Stadium. Mickey Mantle broke for the ball, as did center fielder Joe DiMaggio, who then camped under the ball and called for the catch. Mantle pulled up suddenly, stutter-stepped, and snagged the cleats on his right shoe on a rubber drain cover. His knee buckled, a tendon ripped. Mantle's speed was never the same.

That summer, about 1,400 miles south, in Jonesboro, Arkansas, a similar freak accident—far less publicized—had altered the career of Kyle Rote. The rookie back out of Southern Methodist University, taken No. 1 overall in that summer's NFL Draft, stepped in a hole during a preseason practice at a high school field and tore a knee ligament. Rote, known as "the Mighty Mustang" never fully recovered and became a receiver. "He had an incredible career, considering he did it on one leg," his Giants teammate Frank Gifford once said. "Had he not stepped in the hole, he would be in the Hall of Fame, and I probably wouldn't be."

Born in San Antonio, Rote became an all-state high school basketball and football player. He attended SMU and, in one game, etched his name in Texas gridiron legend. Doak Walker, the 1948 Heisman Trophy winner, was the number-one back for SMU, when Rote was a junior tailback. In the season finale in 1949, Rote stepped in for the injured Walker and grabbed the limelight against Notre Dame, the top-ranked team in the country. Rote ran for 115 yards, threw for 146 yards, averaged 48 yards in punts, and scored all three SMU touchdowns in a 27–20 loss.

"Notre Dame was a 27½-point favorite," he said in an interview with the *Baltimore Sun*. "The oil market was thriving in Texas then. All the oilmen took the points, so from that standpoint we won big.... After the game, a newspaper ran a great headline, 'S.M.U. Wins, 20–27.'"

Twenty-five years later the Fighting Irish later made him an honorary member of its championship team, and the Texas Sportswriters Association voted Rote's performance that afternoon as the greatest by a

Texas athlete in the first half of the century. In the 1949 Cotton Bowl against Oregon, Rote, kicking out of his own end zone, booted a punt that stopped 84 yards from the line of scrimmage, the longest in Cotton Bowl history.

During Rote's senior year, he led the Mustangs to their first No. 1 ranking in 15 years. With 762 rushing yards, 490 in passing, and 13 touchdowns, he was runner-up to Vic Janowicz of Ohio State in the Heisman balloting. By comparison, Walker won the 1948 Heisman with 532 rushing yards and 304 passing. He was elected to the College Hall of Fame in 1964, but as a true mark of his celebrity, Rote had been photographed for the cover of the November 13, 1950, issue of *Life* magazine.

Rote could be considered one of the first "lottery" picks. In January 1951 Giants coach Steve Owen drew a ticket out of a hat that gave the Giants a bonus selection in the college draft, a pick that could be made before the selection process. Rote signed his first Giants contract at Toots Shor's, the Manhattan restaurant renowned as the hangout for sports stars, celebrities, and politicians. It was only his second time in New York.

For the next 11 years, as a flanker and running back, Rote was a real bonus: a captain for 10 of those seasons and four-time Pro Bowler. "He was so good at everything, whether it was Ping-Pong, pool, or kicking off," Giants owner Wellington Mara said when Rote died in 2002. "The outstanding backs of that era were Alex Webster and Frank Gifford. Before Kyle hurt his knee, he was as powerful a runner as Webster was and as smooth a runner and as good a receiver as Gifford was. He just had so much ability."

Nonetheless, his numbers were outstanding: 300 receptions for 4,797 yards and 48 touchdowns, plus 871 rushing yards. His teams were Eastern Conference champions four times and won the title in 1956, knocking off the Chicago Bears. They lost to the Baltimore Colts in the next two seasons and to the Packers in 1961, after which Rote retired.

During those years with the Giants, Gifford said the team had "a lot of animosity" between their offensive and defensive units, and Rote was the only player to bridge that gap. "When he had something to say, it was important," he said. Mara once recalled that Owen sent Rote on the road to scout a game between Chicago and Green Bay.

Rote also helped organize the National Football League Players Association and was its first elected president. His son, Kyle Jr., a pro soccer star, would follow in those footsteps and become a player agent.

Perhaps the most lasting effect of those years was the impact the 1956 team had on the league, Madison Avenue, and the media. "When we won in 1956," Rote recalled, "we won it in Madison Avenue's backyard. These admen, young guys, were bright and sharp, but never had a NFL champion in New York before. Suddenly, they tied it in."

And with the higher visibility, smart, well-spoken, handsome players such as Rote and Gifford became marketable—and employable in the media. Rote was first a sportscaster for local radio—WNEW for eight years—and later as an analyst for NBC for seven years, and would work Super Bowls III and V with Curt Gowdy.

"Every athlete that goes into broadcasting, guys like Pat Summerall and Frank Gifford, owes him a debt of gratitude," linebacker Sam Huff once said. "He really did the first locker room report show by an athlete…at Yankee Stadium. When I was traded to Washington, I copied what he did."

Rote also was backfield coach for the Giants for two years and a Renaissance man: he wrote two books about football, two volumes of poetry, was an ASCAP songwriter, an accomplished pianist, and an oil painter.

Rote "had a great offensive mind regarding the passing game, and football in general," quarterback Y.A. Tittle said. "Everybody liked Kyle Rote. Fans liked him, sportswriters liked him, players liked him. He was just a good person and an outstanding football player."

In fact, according to his son, 14 former Giants—including Jimmy Patton, Don Heinrich, Summerall, and Gifford—named one of their children Kyle.

Mel Hein: "Old Indestructible"

If not for an unusually agreeable postmaster in Providence, Rhode Island, Mel Hein might never have become one of the Giants' most-heralded players—and perhaps the most durable in the history of the game.

Hein was a 60-minute man, an iron man All-America center and defensive lineman at Washington State, but there was no NFL Draft in 1931, and he wasn't recruited. Undeterred, Hein—the Cougars captain who led the team to the Rose Bowl in 1930—wrote to three teams, including the Giants, to express his interest.

The Providence Steam Roller mailed him a contract, which in those days was based on a set amount per game. The Steam Roller offer was $125 a game, and Hein accepted, signing the document and dropping it in the mail. The next day, Hein went to a game in Spokane against Gonzaga, which had been coached in 1930 by Ray Flaherty before he became an assistant coach for the Giants. Flaherty asked if he had received an offer from the Giants.

"No, I haven't," Hein said. "And it's too late, anyway," telling Flaherty about the mailing. When Flaherty told him that the Giants offer was $150 a game, Hein had second thoughts. Flaherty suggested that Hein go to the post office and wire the postmaster in Providence to intercept the letter and ask that it be returned. In a stroke of good fortune, the postmaster obliged, and the next day, Flaherty went to Hein's home with the Giants' contract, and when the Steam Roller contract came back in the mail, Hein ripped it up.

At 6'3" and 230 pounds, Hein wasn't all that much larger than some players in his day. But he was blessed with stamina. He stayed on the field perhaps longer than any player in football history. Hein played both ways in college and in more than 200 regular-season, championship, and exhibition games.

Widely considered the greatest center ever, for eight straight years, from 1933 to 1940, Hein was named the center on the All-NFL team. He received the Joe Carr Trophy as the NFL's Most Valuable Player in 1938; no interior offensive lineman has won it since. In 1963 Hein was the first center to be enshrined in Canton.

A leader by example, Hein played 15 years with the Giants—he was captain for 10—and until age 36, starred on offense and defense thanks to courage, savvy, and great mobility. In fact, he is credited with being both the first center to not simply hold his ground after the snap, but to pull or go downfield and block. He was adept at snapping to any of three backs and occasionally tried a hidden-ball trick, getting the ball back after a semi-snap to quarterback Harry Newman and sneaking down the field.

He also dropped back to cover receivers on defense, which was an innovation. During a late-season win over Green Bay in 1938, he intercepted a pass—one of the 19 in his career—and raced 50 yards to score his only touchdown. Hein had the speed and agility to corner the Packers' top receiver, Don Hutson, on the sideline, but said Bronko Nagurski posed the toughest test. "If you went at him low, he would stomp you to death," Hein recalled. "If you went at him high, he just knocked you down and ran over you."

Giants owner Wellington Mara described Hein as the No. 1 player of the team's first half-century. The only player to come close since was linebacker Lawrence Taylor, considered one of the finest ever at his position.

The records underscore Hein's amazing toughness. In the first half of the 1938 championship game against the Packers, he broke his nose, was knocked out briefly, and was carried off the field but returned a few minutes later. On December 7, 1941, Hein was taken to the hospital in an ambulance after suffering another broken nose and a concussion against the Brooklyn Dodgers. It was the only time he was permanently removed from a game.

Hein, who had helped the Giants win seven Eastern Division championships and two league titles in 1934 and 1938, announced his retirement after the 1941 season to coach at Union College in Schenectady, but the Giants persuaded him to keep playing. For the last four years of his career, Giants head coach Steve Owen allowed him to practice only one day a week. He retired for good after the 1945 season, during which he was the league's highest-paid lineman at $5,000 a year.

In an era when major sports endorsements were rare, Hein had a few. "Nineteen thirty-eight was my big year. I got $150 for endorsing Mayflower Doughnuts," he told *Time* magazine. "When I won the Most Valuable Player award, some pipe company sent me a set of pipes. Free!"

Hein was worth the money. Al Davis, the Raiders' owner and former coach who worked with Hein when both were assistants at the University of Southern California in the 1950s and who later hired him as supervisor of officials for the old American Football League (and later the AFC) in 1965, a position he held until 1974, called him "one of the greatest football players who ever lived."

His teammates were equally laudatory. In 1940 there was a Mel Hein Day at the Polo Grounds, and he received a car and gifts in a pregame ceremony. The Giants lost 14–6 to the Dodgers. Giants teammate Hank Soar said afterward: "We're sorry we didn't win for Mel, but hell, every day the Giants have played in the last 10 years has been Mel Hein Day."

Steve Owen: The Oklahoma Innovator

With an ever-present tobacco chaw and a gravelly Oklahoma drawl, stout Steve Owen wasn't quite the professorial type. Far from it. "Football is a game played down in the dirt, and it always will be. There's no use in getting fancy about it," he often said, and for nine years as a lineman and 23 years as Giants head coach—the longest tenure in franchise history—it was.

Owen, who was born in Native American territory in 1898 and worked on a cattle ranch before playing tackle at Phillips University in Enid, Oklahoma, preached defense and the conservative running game in his career with the Giants, where he compiled a 151–100–17 record, winning eight division titles and two NFL championships as an innovative coach.

After a stint in the Army, a year as coach at Phillips, some jobs in the oil fields, and even some wrestling under the name "Jack O'Brien," Owen agreed in 1924 to play for the barnstorming Kansas City Blues, who later became the Kansas City Cowboys, before folding midway through the 1926 season. Giants owner Tim Mara paid for the Cowboys to play a game in New York, and Owen later agreed to a $500 deal to join the Giants.

Weighing about 260 pounds stacked into a 5'11" frame—it was reported that he once wanted to be a jockey—Owen captained the 1927 team that went 11–1–1 to win the NFL title. That club had 10 shutouts and allowed just 20 points. And Owen was already thinking about ways to improve that performance. In 1931, when he was named coach after two games as co-coach with Benny Friedman in 1930, he unveiled them.

Steve Owen coached the Giants for 23 years, the longest tenure in team history.
Photo courtesy of Getty Images

"Even as a player, Steve tried to convince the coach to use radical departures from the standard five- and six-man lines," Hank Soar told *Football Digest*. "As a coach, he put his ideas into action. We had stunting linemen, rushing linebackers, although we did not call it the blitz, and as the safety man, I often performed what is now called the safety blitz. We had a very good pass defense and fellows like [Sammy] Baugh, [Cecil] Isbell, and [Don] Hutson seldom had good days against us."

In the modern era of the NFL, coaches often substitute players depending on the situation, down, distance, score, and other elements. Owen, however, employed the first such platoons. Under the rules of the 1930s, if a player was taken out, he couldn't return until the next quarter. Coaches started their best 11 players and substituted one-by-one, or when necessary, say, in case of an injury. By the fourth quarter, the starters often were worn out.

So Owen developed two units of similar abilities, one to play to the middle of the first quarter and another to play to the middle of the second, when the rested first group would return.

Owen valued toughness. "If a boy isn't willing to get off the ground and hit back a little harder than he was hit, no coach can help him," he once said. As a coach, he believed strongly in the running game and tin-kered with the traditional single-wing. The A formation—so-called because Owen planned to use a B, C, and D, although he relied almost exclusively on the A—had four men to the right of center Mel Hein and two left. The fullback was four yards behind the center, the quarterback a yard in front of the fullback and to the right. The wingback was posted behind the left end, and the blocking back was a yard back, to the left of Hein, who could snap to any of them.

In that ultraconservative vein, Owen took few chances. "One game I was tackled near the goal and lateraled to 'Tarzan' White who scored a touchdown," Soar said. "Owen pulled me out and gave me hell, he kept reminding me we could have fumbled."

Owen coached in the 1934 NFL Championship Game, known as the "Sneakers Game," when the Giants rebounded after trailing the Bears 13–3 at halftime when they changed from cleats to sneakers at the slippery Polo Grounds and scored 27 straight points. In 1938 the Giants defeated the Green Bay Packers 23–17 for Owen's second title. The Giants won division titles in 1939, 1941, 1944, and 1946, and tied for the American Conference title in 1950, but dropped a playoff game to the Cleveland Browns.

In that 1950 season, Owen developed the "umbrella defense" specif-ically to slow down the Browns' passing attack with quarterback Otto

Graham. From the 6-1-4 or 6-1-2-2 alignment, the ends—Jim Duncan and Ray Poole—would drop back into the flat for pass coverage, leaving four rushers, and the lone linebacker, John Cannady, would specifically shadow the fullback. From the stands, it would look like an opened umbrella.

On October 1, 1950, the Giants shut out the Browns 6–0 and then beat them 17–13 three weeks later. They were the only losses of the season for the Browns. In the playoff game, the Browns scored a mere eight points, but the Giants managed just a field goal.

In 1949 Owen finally—and reluctantly—switched, like most coaches, to the T formation that remains the staple of NFL offenses today, with Charlie Conerly at quarterback.

After he was fired in 1953, the legendary Bears coach George Halas lauded Owen's forward thinking, saying that he "was the first to stress the importance of defense and the advantage of settling for field goals instead of touchdowns. Every team strives today to do what Owen was doing 20 years ago."

Owen coached the Canadian Football League's Toronto Argonauts, the Calgary Stampeders, and Saskatchewan Roughriders, and was named CFL Coach of the Year in 1962.

The United Football League's Syracuse Stormers hired Owen in March 1963, and he was again named a scout for the Giants that November. Owen, unfortunately, suffered a stroke and died on May 17, 1964. The days of the man widely considered the greatest Giants coach were over.

Red and Big Red: Badgro and Webster

In the decades before 1953, the Giants often wore red jerseys with white numbers for home games. For the next 50 years, blue was the sole color for the home jerseys. But in 2004 the red jersey was resurrected as an alternate.

So the color red has some history with "Big Blue"—including as nicknames for two of the club's more notable players: Morris Hiram "Red" Badgro and Alex "Big Red" Webster.

Badgro, who was not the largest of athletes at 6' and 190 pounds, had a fascinating career. A native of Washington State, he attended the

University of Southern California on a basketball scholarship and won 12 letters in football, basketball, and baseball. Badgro and fullback Marion "Duke" Morrison, later known as John Wayne, worked as movie extras, but as Badgro's niece, Dorothy Westland, once said, "Uncle Badge chose football and John chose movies."

In 1927 Badgro began his pro football career with the best-known Red of all, Harold Edward "Red" Grange and the NFL's New York (football) Yankees, which folded after the season. Undaunted, Badgro didn't head to Hollywood like the Duke; he turned to baseball. He was an outfielder for Tulsa in the minors in 1928, and for the St. Louis Browns in 1929 and 1930, hitting .284 and .239.

When the Browns shipped him to the Texas League, coach Steve Owen offered Badgro $150 a game to play for the Giants. "He was a very mild-mannered guy," co-owner Wellington Mara recalled, "but murder on the field. He was a clean player. You had to be because there were only three or four officials, and the other guy could get back at you without the officials catching on…. In those days, players had to supply their own shoes, just as in baseball then. He didn't have money to buy extra football shoes, so he worked out in baseball spikes. Everyone gave him a lot of room so he wouldn't step on their toes. When we scrimmaged, he changed shoes."

Badgro, an All-Pro for four years, played end on both sides of the ball and was highly regarded for his blocking and tackling, although in 1934, he tied for the NFL's pass-catching lead with 16 receptions. He also was the first player to score a touchdown in the first NFL Championship Game in 1933, a 29-yarder from quarterback Harry Newman.

"He could block, catch passes, and would be sick for a week if we lost a ballgame," Owen wrote in his biography, *My Kind of Football.*

On the last play of that title game, with time running out and the Bears ahead 23–21, Badgro caught a pass and sprinted for the goal line. Only Grange, the number-one Red in the NFL, stood between him and the win. Giants Mel Hein and Dale Burnett trailed Badgro, hoping for a lateral, but Grange tackled Badgro high, pinning his arms and brought him down shy of the goal line as time ran out. "Grange's arms were around the ball," Badgro recalled, "and I couldn't get rid of it. If I get by him, we win the game. I wish I had the ball again."

Following the 1935 season, he left to coach and play for the Syracuse team in the American Football League, which disbanded after two games. In 1936 Badgro joined the NFL's Brooklyn Dodgers and then retired. He died at age 95.

As it turned out, Badgro and Chicago Cardinals fullback Ernie Nevers, who pitched for the Browns from 1926 to 1928, were the only two players to be named to All-NFL teams and also play for the Browns.

In a much more important acknowledgment, in 1981, at age 78, Badgro became the oldest inductee into the Pro Football Hall of Fame at the time. "All I knew is that a lot of players were in it who hadn't been All-Pro four times like I had," said Badgro.

* * *

In 1954 the Canadian Football League raided NFL teams, taking the four-time Pro Bowl defensive tackle Arnie Weinmeister from the Giants, who struck back a year later and signed Montreal Alouettes halfback Alex Webster.

Giants offensive guru Vince Lombardi had been unhappy with the blocking of fullback Eddie Price. Webster, a 6'4", 220-pound Kearney, New Jersey, native, had been drafted and cut by the Redskins. He had chosen to go to Canada on a tryout, but Lombardi thought he could fit the bill.

The Giants also drafted Mel Triplett from the University of Toledo in the fifth round that summer. Webster and Triplett led the way for Frank Gifford in many of Lombardi's backfield sets. Gifford and Webster helped the Giants reach six NFL Championship Games from 1956 through 1963.

Webster, who attended North Carolina State, could carry his own weight. From 1955 to 1964 he rushed for 4,638 yards, caught 240 passes for 2,679 yards, and scored 56 touchdowns (39 rushing and 17 receiving). Webster made five catches for 76 yards and scored two touchdowns on short runs in a 47–7 rout of the Chicago Bears in the 1956 title game and was named to the Pro Bowl in 1958 and 1961.

Webster also had a rep as a partier who was comfortable in the Manhattan nightlife. "He was always amazing to me," Gifford once said. "He was always in the worst shape of anyone who ever played, probably. He smoked and drank, not to excess, and then he'd come out and play a whole game and run over people. He was one tough dude." Colts defensive star Gino Marchetti called Webster, according to writer Don Smith, "the toughest guy I ever played against." Strange, because Webster didn't appear to be that way off the field. Smith knew him as "big, burly, docile, nice."

But everybody, even fans, knew that Webster was a smoker, an addiction that he knew was a significant health issue. When he later coached the Giants from 1969 to 1973, Webster smoked on the sideline. "Cigarettes were my downfall," he told Florida newspapers after he retired. "I always wondered that sometimes when I ran out of gas, if I hadn't smoked whether I could've kept on going."

He himself wondered if the tank was empty when he picked up Kyle Rote's fumble in the seesaw 1958 championship game against the Colts and ran it 65 yards to the 1-yard line when he was tackled from behind and fell into the end zone. Officials spotted the ball on the 1, and Triplett went over for a 14–10 lead. Webster later said, "If only I had a little more speed, I would've made it easily." The Colts would win that game—the first nationally televised title game in history—23–17 in overtime.

Webster spent a few seasons as an assistant coach and a broadcaster in the Giants radio booth until 1968, when former teammate Dick Lynch succeeded him. In 1969 the Giants lost all five of their exhibition games, including a 37–14 trouncing by the Super Bowl III–champion Jets, who had become an upstart, crosstown rival. Co-owner Wellington Mara had had enough; he fired Allie Sherman and named Webster head coach.

As a coach, Webster wasn't a disciplinarian, and would only see "red" with rage occasionally. He was named NFL Coach of the Year in 1970, when the Fran Tarkenton–led Giants finished with a 9–5 record but didn't make the playoffs. Nor did they before he resigned after a 2–11–1 campaign in 1973. His overall record was 29–40–1.

The glory days of the Giants, like Webster and Badgro, two Reds in the annals of Big Blue, had faded to gray.

Roosevelt "Rosey" Brown

Pro scouts today have an armada of technology at their fingertips—from Google to advanced medical testing to DVDs of high school and college games. None of that existed when Roosevelt Brown was playing in college in the early 1950s. When the Giants drafted Brown out of Morgan State University in Baltimore in the 27th of 30 rounds, they weren't ashamed to admit that they hardly had heard of him. Few had. No franchise had the time or the money to dig that deep.

The Giants learned about Brown the old-fashioned way—from a newspaper. Someone spotted a reference to Brown, who was born in Charlottesville, Virginia, in the *Pittsburgh Courier*, a weekly, in an article about selections to the 1952 Black All-America team. "We had nothing to lose," said Wellington Mara, who was in charge of personnel at the time.

Oh, but the did the Giants ever have a lot to gain.

Brown, the two-time captain of the Morgan State wrestling team, also lettered in baseball. The son of a railroad worker, he was 6'3" and weighed 255 pounds, but sported a 29-inch waist. The only reason he went out for football, as Brown told it, was because "my high school coach thought I was too big to be playing trombone in the school band."

Having signed a contract for about $3,000, the 21-year-old Brown arrived by train to Giants camp at a college in Minnesota in a dark suit, wearing a homburg and carrying a cardboard suitcase and an umbrella. Brown had never played against white players, so camp was an adjustment, but he succeeded.

Given his size, Steve Owen and Jim Lee Howell, the Giants' coaches, initially used Brown on the defensive front in goal-line situations. Before long, however, Brown's combination of power and speed made them reassess that decision. In fact, they redrew part of their playbook when they installed him at left tackle, where he flourished as the first "pulling tackle" on sweeps, leading backs such as Alex Webster and Frank Gifford across the line of scrimmage and beyond.

"Our two favorite plays were 48 pitchout and [Vince] Lombardi's 49 sweep, and Rosie was the key man in all of that," Gifford recalled after Brown died at age 71 in 2004. "The longest run in my career [79 yards] was on a 48 pitchout against Washington. Rosie made a block at the line of scrimmage. I cut it up, and then I'm running downfield and I look up and I see No. 79 [Brown] in front of me, and he wiped out another guy. Rosey would've been a tight end in today's game because he was such a great athlete and had such great speed for a man his size."

Brown also was durable. He missed just four of 166 regular-season games in his NFL career. "He was a big Jim Brown," linebacker Sam Huff said. "When I came to the Giants training camp from the College All-Star Game in 1956 and I saw Roosevelt Brown sitting outside the dormitory in Winooski, Vermont, in a T-shirt and shorts, I wanted to turn around and go back to West Virginia. I said, 'Are they all built like this?' He and I played on all the special teams, and he was faster than me."

Huff also recalled Brown's humor. "When I was a rookie, he said, 'Do you have any money?' I said, 'I have $10.' And he said, 'Loan it to me.' He never paid me back until I made the team. When I made the team, I said, 'Where's my $10?' He said, 'I'd better pay you because you made the team. I thought you were going to get cut.'"

In a career that spanned 1953 to 1965, he was an eight-time All-Pro and selected to play in the Pro Bowl on nine occasions. No question, Brown was a cornerstone in one of the glorious eras of the 84-year-old franchise. In 1956 Brown was voted Lineman of the Year when the Giants won the NFL title. In the 1956 championship game against the Bears, he did a superb job on defensive end Ed Meadows, and the Giants won 47–7. Brown's teams also won six division titles.

Brown was a member of the league's 75th Anniversary All-Time Team (selected in 1994), and the 2000 All-Time Team chosen by members of the Hall of Fame selection committee. A fearless pass blocker for quarterbacks Charlie Conerly and Y.A. Tittle, as well, Brown, along with Forrest Gregg, Jim Parker, and Anthony Munoz, ranks in the top all-time at his position.

When phlebitis forced Brown to hang up the cleats, he became the Giants' assistant offensive line coach in 1966, and the offensive line coach in 1969. He joined the scouting department in 1971, where he worked until his death. He was inducted in the Hall of Fame in 1975.

At training camps—often alongside Wellington Mara—he observed the linemen going through drills and helped the front office in draft preparation. Ernie Accorsi, the longtime football executive who worked with Brown as a Giant, recalled one draft-day moment. "Rosey gave a spontaneous philosophical talk," said Accorsi. "If it was recorded, it would be a manuscript for how to conduct a draft, a manuscript on scouting, on how to get these kids to become a finished product. He was a very wise man."

Ken Strong: Strength in Two Sports

His prowess in football is well-documented: from a magnificent college player praised by the legendary sportswriter Grantland Rice to an NFL star who scored two touchdowns and kicked a field goal in the "Sneakers Game" when the Giants switched shoes for the second half in the icy championship game at the Polo Grounds and scored four touchdowns to top the Bears 30–13 in December 1934.

But Strong could very well have been a feared major league baseball player as well. The Yankees signed Strong in June 1929 before he graduated from New York University, and the power-hitting prospect trained with the team in Florida. He was assigned to New Haven and played a year there, hitting 21 homers. In Hazelton, Pennsylvania, the next season, he belted 41 homers—a New York–Penn League record until recently—and drove in 130 runs. In one game, he hit four home runs in consecutive at-bats.

In 1931 he played right field for the Yankees' Toronto Maple Leafs affiliate and hit .342 with nine homers. During a night game in Buffalo, however, an injury and subsequent botched surgery wrecked the out-fielder's major league dream. On a deep fly, Strong had raced back, caught the ball, and hit the center-field fence. A bone chipped in his right wrist, but it was diagnosed as a sprain, and he played out the season.

The Tigers reportedly considered Strong a better prospect than future Hall of Famer Hank Greenberg, who they would later acquire, and purchased his contract in the 1932 winter meetings. The Yanks received $40,000 and five players. When Strong finally underwent the wrist operation, the surgeon removed a bone rather than the floating chip, according to his family, and left him with no flexibility and a weak throwing motion.

Fassel: A Coach for Life

Jim Fassel is a lifer. After decades of coaching, in 2009 he signed up to coach the Las Vegas team in the United Football League. Here's one of his takes on the job at the end of the line with the Giants. "There are a lot of people around me who always tell me, 'You don't realize what you go through,'" he said. "'There is another side of life that you don't even see.' I think back on it. I know from a family standpoint and all of that stuff, I mean for seven years [coaching] has taken up the biggest bulk of my time. I have spent more time in my office than I have at my house. You don't realize it. I look back over my career and there are some things that I missed with my family that had to do with the hours of coaching. You have to love it. I had a coach one time ask me about coaching. He said, 'If you can do without it, then do it.' Unless you love it…it beats you down, it wears you down, but I don't look at life that way. I mean, if you want to look at coaching as a profession of what happens to some people, you could paint a very negative picture of why you would coach. That is why you have to have a passion for what you do, and I do. It was like John Elway when I was talking to him about when he retired—if I am waiting for the day that I don't want to coach on Sunday, that will never happen. I'd do that for the rest of my life. But it is the grind and the wearing-down process, the pounding on you and the hours you put in. What is different about coaching is that you put your whole life into the week."

Strong could still play football quite well, however. At 6' and 205 pounds, he once ran the 100—in equipment—in 10 seconds. As a senior halfback at NYU in 1928, he ran for 2,100 yards and, including his kicks, led the country in scoring with 162 of his team's 316 points. In three varsity seasons, Strong had 34 touchdowns, 66 extra points, and five field goals for 285 points.

In one epic 1928 game against Carnegie Tech, one of the best programs in the nation, Strong excelled. Down 7–0, Strong scored all of NYU's points. He threw two long touchdown passes, ran for touchdowns of 43 and 14 yards, and kicked three extra points in a 27–13 win. "This attack was led by a runaway buffalo, using the speed of a deer, and his name was Ken Strong," Rice wrote. "He ran all over a big, powerful team, smashed its line, ran its ends, kicked 50 and 55 yards, threw passes, and tackled all over the lot. Today he was George Gipp, Red Grange, and Chris Cagle rolled into one human form, and there was nothing Carnegie had that could stop his march."

After college, Strong—who was born in West Haven, Connecticut—was strongly pursued by the Giants. He turned down a $3,000 contract from coach LeRoy Andrews and joined the NFL's Staten Island Stapletons, where he scored over 45 percent of the team's points over four years.

The Stapletons folded after the 1932 season, and Strong eventually accepted that $3,000 offer. With his multiple talents, Strong helped guide the Giants to Eastern Division titles in 1933 and 1934, scoring in each title game. He tied for the league lead with 64 points in 1933.

In 1933 he also became the first player in NFL history to officially attempt and score on a fair-catch kick, on November 20 against the Green Bay Packers. It was from 30 yards out. Only three other players have made successful fair-catch kicks in the NFL—the Packers' Paul Hornung on September 13, 1964 (52 yards); the Vikings' Fred Cox on December 4, 1966 (40); and Mac Percival of the Bears (43) on November 3, 1968.

Strong's financial issues with the Giants and the NFL continued to mount. He hired a lawyer to win a salary increase to $6,000 the next season. Then, after the 1935 season, the NFL instituted the college draft, which provided a bounty of low-cost bodies. The Giants offered Strong $150 a game, a pitch he rejected and inked a $5,000 deal with the New York Yankees of the fledgling American Football League.

The AFL folded after two years, but the NFL hammered Strong for his defection. "Extreme disloyalty," it was termed, and the league suspended him for five years. The Giants sent him to their farm team in Jersey City, New Jersey. After the 1939 season, at age 33, Strong retired.

Oddly enough, that would not be the last of Strong's career with the Giants. Four years later, when World War II eroded NFL rosters, Strong was sought out by the Giants and kicked for four seasons, through 1947. This time, he exercised some leverage, and the team allowed him to wear no shoulder pads and even a wristwatch. However equipped, Strong made 18 field goals and converted 102 of 104 extra points.

After the 1947 season, he retired for good at age 41. He had scored 484 points in 12 NFL seasons, and his 351 points were a Giants record until Frank Gifford broke that mark in the 1950s. Twenty years after he retired, Strong was inducted into the Pro Football Hall of Fame. He died in 1979.

Y.A. Tittle: Old-School All the Way

When the San Francisco 49ers, under coach Red Hickey, decided to turn to a new shotgun offense, it was determined that quarterback Y.A. Tittle—somewhat less than nimble—didn't suit the style of a quarterback several yards behind scrimmage.

So, in the blockbuster trade of 1961, the 13-year veteran was sent to the Giants for second-year offensive lineman Lou Cordileone, a Jersey City, New Jersey, native who attended Clemson. If the name doesn't ring a bell, you're excused.

Both Tittle, the starter since 1952, and Cordileone were stunned. When Allie Sherman, then the Giants' coach, called Cordileone into his office to inform him, Cordileone asked, "What other players are in the deal?"

"Nobody else," Sherman said.

"Me for Tittle?" asked Cordileone. "Just me?"

Cordileone had every right to be shocked. After all, in most of those 13 seasons, Yelberton Abraham Tittle was among the top five quarterbacks in the league in categories such as passing yardage, attempts, completions, and yards per game.

Growing up in Marshall, Texas, Tittle's hero was Slingin' Sammy Baugh. "I remember playing catch in the yard all by myself while listening to Sammy play on the radio," Tittle once recalled. "I thought he could never lose a game. In 1952 Baugh's last season as a player, we went to Washington and beat them 23–17. I never felt so bad winning a game."

In four years with the Giants, Tittle would feel good—most of the time. He was brought to New York to replace the popular and effective Charlie Conerly, who was 40, not an easy task. But Tittle led the Giants to three straight NFL title games and was named Player of the Year each season.

In his first appearance, on September 24, 1961, in Forbes Field, Tittle relieved Conerly and completed 10 of 12 passes, including a five-yard touchdown to Joe Morrison that proved to be the game-winner in a 17–14 victory over the Steelers.

Over four years with the Giants, Tittle would have a 32–13–2 won-lost record, 96 touchdowns, and 10,439 yards.

Although Tittle never won an NFL championship, his most memorable game came on October 28, 1962. There was little to detect that this October day at Yankee Stadium would be anything so historic. Six of his first seven passes fell incomplete. In fact, Tittle had injured his arm against the Lions the previous week. But then, everything clicked, touchdown after touchdown. Seven of them: Joe Morrison for 22 yards, Joe Walton from 5 in the second quarter, one yard to Morrison again right before the half.

The second half began with a 53-yarder to his roommate, Del Shofner, who finished with 11 catches for 269 yards. The roommates had developed chemistry. The willowy Shofner, who brought his blazing speed to New York in 1961 for a first-round draft pick from the Rams, led the team in receiving each of the next three campaigns. With Tittle throwing, Shofner scored 32 touchdowns in the league's most feared passing offense.

Tittle then found Walton again for 26 yards and Frank Gifford for a long, 63-yard score. For the seventh TD, Walton and Gifford crisscrossed from the right side, and Walton made the catch six yards away by the flag. With the completion, Tittle tied Sid Luckman, Adrian Burk, and later Joe Kapp, for the most touchdown passes in an NFL game. The Oilers' George Blanda had seven in an AFL game.

His 505 yards in the 49–34 win was a team record until Phil Simms connected for 513 in 1985. If anything, Tittle was a throwback: he kept wearing his old high-top shoes when everyone else had switched to low-cut ones, he wore the same pair of leather shoulder pads throughout his 17 seasons, and he sat in the same seat in the back of the team bus. "I had all kinds of little rituals that were sort of stupid," he once recalled.

Whatever they were, it didn't hurt.

As a Giant, Tittle continued to impress. He set an NFL record by throwing 36 touchdown passes during the 1963 season. But the championship game on December 29 of that year finally began his road to retirement.

At Wrigley Field, the day started well with Tittle's 14-yard touchdown to Frank Gifford. Later in the first period, Tittle injured his left knee when Larry Morris hit him during his throwing motion. Morris then intercepted Tittle's screen pass and returned the ball 61 yards to the

Perhaps the most famous photograph in NFL history, the image of a bloody Y.A. Tittle during a 1964 game against the Steelers captured the rough, violent nature of the game.

Giants' 5-yard line. Morris reinjured Tittle's knee in the second quarter, and head coach Allie Sherman did not trust little-used backup Glynn Griffing, even punting on third down.

Taped and medicated with painkillers, Tittle was forced to throw off his back foot and threw four more interceptions.

For all practical purposes, the Tittle era ended at Pitt Stadium in Pittsburgh on September 20, 1964. Deep in Giants territory in the second quarter, Tittle looked left as the offense set up a screen for Morrison. Unbeknownst to the balding, 38-year-old veteran, Steelers defensive end John Baker had beaten tackle Lane Howell and bore down. Baker plowed into Tittle with his left shoulder and right arm just as he aimed a pass, lifting the signal-caller off the ground. The force of the blow knocked Tittle to his knees, and his helmet bounced off when he hit the turf. Chuck Hinton intercepted the floater as Tittle, bloodied and dazed, watched from the end-zone grass. Murray Berman's award-winning photo captured the moment better than any words.

Gasping for breath, Tittle was helped to the locker room. "It looked like my head was hurting, but it was actually my rib cage. I pulled cartilage," he said. "My head was bleeding because my helmet cut it when I hit the ground." A 14–0 lead was gone. The Steelers survived and won 27–24, and although Tittle played in every game that season, the Giants would win only two.

In 1964 Tittle retired after a career lasting 17 years, which included 33,070 passing yards and 242 touchdowns. His No. 14 was retired and, justifiably, Tittle was inducted into the Pro Football Hall of Fame in 1971.

chapter 6

The Great Eight

For eight years, from 1956 to 1963, the roll call was simply astounding: Frank Gifford, Pat Summerall, Charlie Conerly, Andy Robustelli, Sam Huff, Rosey Brown, Rosey Grier, Kyle Rote, Alex Webster, Vince Lombardi, Tom Landry, Jim Lee Howell, Allie Sherman, Jim Katcavage, Harland Svare.

They were the toast of the town and of NFL lore. Their games, stories, and memories have been heavily chronicled in documentaries and on television (Gifford and Summerall, of course, enjoyed lengthy, high-profile NFL broadcasting careers), on DVDs, in many well-written books and autobiographies, and in countless newspaper and magazine articles. Their relationships with the media and fans continued long after their playing and coaching careers ended.

If those eight years—which included six championship-game appearances—were the peak for the storied franchise, the next two decades would be the valley, the chasm, the black hole. Four wins, 10 losses in 1971. Then nomads. Playing poorly in the Yale Bowl in 1973. Winning two games in 1974. Five-and-nine in 1975, when Shea Stadium was their temporary home. Three-and-11 in the inaugural season at Giants Stadium in East Rutherford, New Jersey. On and on. Five-and-nine in 1977. Four-and-12 in 1980. LT arrives in 1981, and there is a ray of hope, a cornerstone on which to build championships, but not before a 3–12–1 thud in 1983. Twenty lost seasons.

Plenty of stories, many unpleasant and forgettable, arose from those darker years.

These are just some of the ones from the Great Eight.

Starting in 1950, the pieces began to fall into place for a stirring era. The Giants and New York Bulldogs divided the players of the former All-American Football Conference Yankees. The Giants received Tom Landry, a young defensive back from Texas, and a defensive tackle from Washington, Arnie Weinmeister, who would be a three-time All-Pro. Rote was drafted in 1951; Gifford was the No. 1 overall pick from USC in 1952. Morgan State's Brown was the Giants' 27th pick the following year. In 1954 Howell, a former ends coach, replaced Steve Owen, who had been head coach for 23 years.

Owen, a former tackle, was a down-home Oklahoman and defensive thinker. He was the first known coach to elect to kick off rather than receive on the opening coin toss to allow his pumped-up defense to be on the field first. He would substitute entire units each quarter. And he fashioned the 6-1-4 or "umbrella" defense, using Landry and the future Hall of Fame safety Emlen Tunnell as the deep men. In the 6-1-4, the ends peeled back toward the sidelines, creating a prototype 4-3 for pass coverage. It totally stymied Otto Graham in Cleveland's home opener at Municipal Stadium on October 1, 1950. The great quarterback was 12-for-30 with three interceptions.

The search for building blocks continued. Also in 1954, during a contract war with the Canadian Football League that cost the Giants the services of Weinmeister, Wellington Mara signed the CFL's best player, Montreal Alouettes halfback Alex Webster.

Two years later, in 1956, Andy Robustelli, a down-and-dirty defensive end, was obtained from the Los Angeles Rams. A World War II combat vet, a graduate of Arnold College, undersized, and nearing age 30, Robustelli anchored a Giants defensive unit so fierce and relentless that they were the first team to inspire crowds to chant, "Dee-fense!" when the team moved into Yankee Stadium.

The 1956 Championship Season

In their inaugural season in the Bronx, the Giants would win their first title in 18 years. The Bears and the Giants had played in the first "Sneakers Game" 22 years ago, when the Giants—using borrowed pairs of rubber-soled basketball shoes from Manhattan college on the slick field of the icy Polo Grounds for the second half—cut and juked and left Chicago defenders in their wake, scoring 27 points in the final quarter.

This time, on December 30, 1956, at Yankee Stadium, the Bears were prepared—sort of. They brought worn-out sneakers; the Giants had brand-new ones supplied by Robustelli's sporting goods store. The telltale sign, the portent of things to come, came quickly. On the opening kickoff, halfback Gene Filipski glided behind his blockers and brought the ball back 53 yards. Four plays later from the 17, Mel Triplett, similarly shod, burst up the middle, pushed an umpire at the 5 ahead of him, and fell on him in the end zone, along with two Bears tacklers.

On the next Bears drive, Robustelli recovered a fumble. A field goal followed, and Jimmy Patton intercepted a pass that led to another field goal. Webster scored on two short runs and the rout was on, 34–7 at halftime. The Giants won 47–7, adding to the Bears' misery with Conerly TD passes to Rote and Gifford.

Gifford had four receptions for 131 yards and a touchdown and ran for 30 more. Webster had five catches for 76 yards while rushing for two scores. "Winning that game," Webster would say later, "made us win for the next six or seven years." After four championship game losses, the Giants were back in title territory.

Actually, the Giants didn't win in 1957, but Gifford finished in the top 10 in both receiving (fourth) and rushing (10th), with 588 yards receiving and 528 yards rushing. Gifford also completed 4 of 6 passes for 143 yards and two touchdowns.

Missing the Vet

To be sure, players have different perceptions of opposing stadiums. Lincoln Financial Field replaced Veterans Stadium in Philadelphia, which was infamous for its drunken, rowdy fan behavior. Michael Strahan called Eagles fans "the meanest of all."

But Pennsylvania native Kerry Collins didn't mind, possibly because of a childhood memory rather than some particularly vulgar boos. "The Vet was a special place," the quarterback said. "That was a pretty hard place to play. I am sure the Linc will be loud and they will be obnoxious and all of that kind of stuff. Philly has some very passionate fans. I miss the Vet. When I was in Little League, we actually took infield on the Vet before a Phillies game."

"The Greatest Game Ever Played" and Its Preludes

In 1958 the game that got all the pub was the championship against the Colts at Yankee Stadium, likely to be referred to forever as "the Greatest Game Ever Played," largely because it featured so many major stars and was the first sudden-death overtime in a title game.

But four Giants games that led up to the 23–17 Baltimore win had some fascinating subplots. Here they are, in snapshots, one in November and three in December.

In front of 71,163 at Yankee Stadium on November 9, the Giants caught a break. The 6–0 Colts were without injured quarterback Johnny Unitas. Baltimore backup George Shaw threw for three touchdowns, but it was Frank Gifford's arm—and legs—that ended their unbeaten string. Gifford threw a halfback option from Charlie Conerly on the first play from scrimmage to Bob Schnelker for a 63-yard gain that led to a touchdown. Gifford then scored on a 13-yard sweep in the third quarter. With 2:40 to play, Pat Summerall kicked a game-winning 28-yard field goal for a 24–21 decision.

On December 7, against the Lions in Detroit, the Giants hung on thanks to a stunt by Robustelli and Harland Svare to block a field-goal attempt with 1:21 to play that might have won the game. Tobin Rote passes and a fake punt by Yale Lary were the key plays in giving the Lions a 17–12 lead. But Gifford scored to put the Giants on top 19–17. Jim Martin lined up from the 25, and Svare told Robustelli, "I'll block the kick. You have a better blocking angle. You drive him inside." Robustelli muscled lineman Gerald Perry inside, Svare hit the gap with arms extended, and the ball struck his extended left hand.

The Browns were 9–2, the Giants 8–3, and on December 14, the Giants needed a victory to force a playoff game. It was like a game played in a snow globe called Yankee Stadium. Cleveland's ground game dominated, with Jim Brown rushing for 148 yards, including a 65-yard touchdown early. Giants kicker Pat Summerall had made a field goal, but missed a 46-yarder and a 32-yarder in the inclement weather, the last with just over four minutes to play. It was 10–10, and the snow continued to swirl. The ball was on the Cleveland 49 with 2:07 left.

Summerall recounted the story many times. It was fourth down, and Coach Howell summoned Summerall to make the attempt. "I

Charlie Conerly, Alex Webster, and Frank Gifford completed a double handoff and lateral to beat the Browns for the 1958 Eastern Division championship.

couldn't believe Jim Lee was asking me," said Summerall. "That was the longest attempt I ever made for the Giants. It was a bad field and unrealistic. The guys on the bench didn't believe it. They wanted another pass." When he got to the huddle, Summerall was greeted unceremoniously by his roommate, Conerly. "What the hell are you doing here?" Conerly asked.

Summerall lined up straight behind the spot, Conerly put the ball down, and it sailed through the uprights. Summerall was mobbed by his teammates. "You son of a bitch, you know you can't kick it that far," offensive coordinator Vince Lombardi told him afterward. What is often forgotten in all the hoopla was that Lou Groza's 55-yarder with 25 seconds left fell short. Or there never would have been a "Greatest Game."

A week later, it was Giants-Browns II. In the previous game, Brown, who had gained an NFL-record 1,527 yards rushing, had run 26 times and was basically unstoppable. The mission for the defense: stop him at all costs. The task fell to the Giants' 4-3 defense: Katcavage and Robustelli on each end and Grier and Dick Modzelewski at tackles. Ideally, the plays would funnel to linebackers Huff, Svare, and Cliff Livingston. Landry, Tunnell, and Patton were the horses in the secondary. (Dick Lynch came aboard in 1959; Erich Barnes in 1961.) Never before was Brown so locked down. He was held to just eight yards on seven carries, the lowest total of his career.

On offense, it came down to one play, a reverse designed by Lombardi, the offensive coordinator, which the team practiced all week. But there was a twist. And it involved Chuckin' Charlie Conerly. Conerly had been acquired in a 1948 trade with Washington for Howie Livingston and initially didn't prosper under Steve Owen, who preached defense and an A formation. A tailback at Ole Miss, Conerly was a quarterback in the pros, and with the Giants not only was he sacked often, he was taunted by fans who held signs like "Back to the Farm." In 1954 he began thriving in Lombardi's offense and took full advantage of what New York offered: the clubs, the restaurants, the nightlife. Marlboro used him in their cowboy-themed ads as a "Marlboro Man." In 1959 Conerly was league MVP and led everyone in passing. Before his No. 42 was retired, he would engineer 20 fourth-quarter comebacks and throw for more than 19,000 yards.

On this play, as drawn up, Conerly would hand the ball off. Webster would run left, while guard Al Berry and Gifford went to the right and Gifford would take the ball from Webster. It all went as planned in the first quarter, until Gifford saw Bob Gain and Galen Fiss closing in. He first faked a lateral and then did lateral to a surprised Conerly on the sideline at the 10-yard line. The 37-year-old Conerly took off, was hit by safety Junior Wren, but dove in for the touchdown. The Giants held the Browns to 86 total yards in a 10–0 shutout.

"The reverse didn't surprise me, but the lateral to Conerly?" blustered Cleveland coach Paul Brown. "They couldn't have planned it. What the hell was he doing there?"

Said Conerly, "I was supposed to be there if Gifford needed me," said Conerly. "I don't know how long it had been since I scored a touchdown, but it was great for an old guy like me."

• • •

Lights, camera, action. NBC showed the December 28, 1958, championship game to the world. Chris Schenkel was the play-by-play man.

Colts back Alan Ameche scored the winning touchdown in overtime of the 1958 NFL Championship Game, also known as "the Greatest Game Ever Played."

Bob Wolff was on the radio. Summerall's first-quarter, 36-yard field goal was trumped by Colts running back Alan Ameche's two-yard touchdown after Gifford's first fumble of the second quarter. A Unitas-to–Raymond Berry 15-yarder after Gifford's second fumble made it 14–3 at halftime.

In the third quarter, Ameche was stopped twice from the 1-yard line, the second time by Cliff Livingston on an fourth-down option five yards behind scrimmage. Triplett capped a 95-yard drive with a one-yard run to cut the lead to 14–10. The highlight play of that drive was Webster's recovery of a Kyle Rote fumble after Conerly completed a pass to him around midfield from the 14. Rote broke an arm-tackle but was tackled from behind, and Webster, trailing, scooped up the ball and rambled to the 1, where he was knocked out of bounds.

The 64,185 fans exploded when Gifford caught a 15-yard toss from Conerly in the fourth quarter. But with less than two minutes left, the

Colts took over at their own 14-yard line and Unitas guided to Colts to the Giants 13-yard line, where Steve Myhra's 20-yard kick with seven seconds left sent the game into overtime—the first in NFL history. "When the game ended in a tie, we were standing on the sidelines waiting to see what came next," Unitas said later. "The officials came over and said, 'Send the captain out. We're going to flip a coin to see who will receive.' That was the first we heard of the overtime period."

The Giants took the kickoff but were forced to punt, and Baltimore drove 80 yards on 13 plays and scored on Ameche's one-yard run to win it 23–17. The rematch next season was less of a classic.

In 1959 the Colts would score 24 fourth-quarter points in the title game against the Giants for their second consecutive championship.

The Hit

For the Giants, the new decade began on a sour note. Tim Mara had died in 1959, and Chuck Bednarik almost killed Gifford. On November 20, 1960, the Eagles came to Yankee Stadium, and Bednarik, an uncompromising linebacker and center, leveled Gifford on a third-and-10 play, separating him from the ball. Gifford's head bounced off the turf, and he lay unconscious. Chuck Weber recovered, and Bednarik celebrated. "I hit him good and I hit him clean," he said. "In this game, a man can get hurt."

Gifford, who would not play again for a year and a half, would not remember any of it. "I just saw the replay more times than the *Hindenburg* disaster," he said.

Bednarik, a Bethlehem, Pennsylvania, native who had been an Air Force gunner and flew 30 combat missions over Germany, was vilified for what was perceived as celebrating unnecessarily. His explanation: "He was doing a down-and-in pattern, and I saw him coming; I just hit him high in the chest about as hard as I could. His head snapped, and he went flying one way, and the ball went flying another. Since I was following the ball, I didn't know where Gifford had gone. One of our linebackers, Chuck Weber, was scrambling to get the ball. My eyes were closed and my hands clenched, and I just happened to turn around. Unbeknownst to me, Gifford was lying on the ground, unconscious.

Sock Checks

Two inches below the knee? Straighten that out.

You've heard of bed checks for curfew? How about sock checks?

"Everything has to be perfect," said linebacker Nick Greisen in camp in 2004. "With Coach Fassel you might have been able to get away with a couple things here and there, but Coach Coughlin will be looking at your socks to make sure they are the same level, and that's the great thing about him. He is not going to let one guy get away with anything, because if he lets a veteran get away with something, then other guys try to get away with things too."

I had no idea he was there. There's another photo in which I'm crouching down to make sure he is all right.... It will never die, and not because it helped us beat the Giants 17–10 in an important game. People remember that hit for two reasons. First, I tell people that if you do anything big, do it in New York. And second, since it happened to a revered guy like Frank, it'll never die. If that tackle was against anybody else, in any other city, it would have been forgotten."

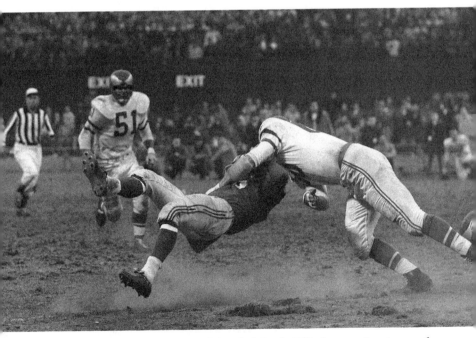

Eagles linebacker Chuck Bednarik knocked Frank Gifford unconscious in one of the most famous and brutal plays in NFL history. Photo courtesy of Getty Images

The Pete Previte Special

If you scan the tapes and talk to those who were there, there were so many memorable games and plays in 1961. Erich Barnes returned an interception 102 yards against the Cowboys on October 15; Conerly, at 40, threw two touchdowns in the last four minutes to beat the Rams 24–14 on October 22 and three touchdowns on December 10 in a 28–24 comeback over the Eagles.

A personal favorite? The Pete Previte Special.

Previte was a Yankee Stadium clubhouse attendant/equipment manager who loved baseball and football. On November 12, 1961, he suggested "pinch-hitting" the speedy secondary mates, Barnes and Jimmy Patton, on offense to create a five-receiver spread with Tittle in the shotgun in a game against the Eagles.

With the Giants up 17–7 and about a minute to go in the half, the coaching staff agreed. Why not? On the left, Barnes and Del Shofner went deep, and Shofner was double-covered. Patton, Rote, and Joe Walton were on the right side, running shorter patterns. Barnes caught a 62-yarder running a post from the left against Maxie Baughan and sped to paydirt for the 24–7 lead.

This all came in the first years of Brooklyn-born head coach Allie Sherman, who had been offensive coordinator. He replaced Jim Lee Howell after Lombardi, who had departed for Green Bay in 1959 and couldn't be lured back. The Giants won the Eastern Division in 1961, 1962, and 1963, and Sherman was named Coach of the Year in the first two, despite losing to Lombardi's Packers in the title games.

Ah, Experience

It really separates the men from the boys in training camp.

When the Giants trained in Albany, New York, Antonio Pierce, who had arrived from Washington the previous season, was prepared for camp number two upstate. Pierce had all the essentials. "I brought better comforters," he said. "You know the little eggshell thing, a little more comfort on that bed. TVs, I always bought the TVs, but as long as you got your chargers and all your toothbrushes and toothpaste and all the little things…. I didn't bring that much because if you bring it, you gotta unpack it."

Sherman knew the vagaries of the New York fans. When you win, you're idolized. Lose, and you're a bum. So, when he began trading aging veterans like Huff and the team stumbled to a 24–43–3 record through 1968, the "Good-bye Allie" chants rained down from Yankee Stadium. Sherman was axed during the preseason in 1969.

Oh-So-Close in '63

Summerall retired in 1962, but the Giants still had Gifford, and he would be the catalyst in winning the Eastern Division title on the final day of the 1963 season against the Steelers at Yankee Stadium. The 10–3 Giants were up 16–10 in the third quarter and faced a third-and-8 on their own 24. With Gifford catching sideline passes most of the day, Tittle called a wing zing-in. Gifford, flanked right, would drop his shoulder as if to head to the sideline again but slant over the middle. Pittsburgh's Glenn Glass bit, but Tittle's throw was low. Somehow, Gifford pulled it in with one hand, turned upfield, and Glass caught him at the Steelers 47.

"It was the biggest catch I ever made," Gifford said later. "All I was trying to do was bat the ball up in the air and it stuck in my hand." Joe Morrison later snared a 22-yarder for a touchdown, and the game was essentially over. The Giants advanced with a 33–17 triumph but lost to the Bears in the championship game, 14–10.

chapter 7

A Legacy of Defense

Jesse Armstead

With one play, linebacker Jesse Armstead almost turned around Super Bowl XXXV in 2001 against the Baltimore Ravens.

With the Ravens holding a 7–0 lead early in the second quarter, Trent Dilfer attempted a screen pass to Jamal Lewis that was intercepted by Armstead and returned for an apparent touchdown. The play was called back for a questionable defensive holding call on Keith Hamilton. Whatever momentum the Giants might have mustered just vanished, the Ravens forced some turnovers, built a lead, and went on to win 34–7.

"All I remember is hitting Dilfer, and I saw he dumped it and I just heard the crowd and I look up and there is Jessie running like he stole something," recalled defensive end Michael Strahan. "That really, I think, put a damper in our Super Bowl. But at the same time, I was proud to be on a team with all of those guys, with Jessie, that we went that far."

Born in 1970 in Dallas, Texas, Armstead was a college standout on Miami's national championship teams with Warren Sapp and Ray Lewis, but he tore his anterior cruciate ligament in his sophomore season and wasn't drafted until the eighth round in 1993, when he was selected by the Giants and really blossomed.

Armstead, who played nine years with the Giants before leaving in 2002 when he was signed to a three-year, $4.5 million deal by the Redskins, was a five-time Pro Bowl linebacker between 1997 and 2001. He had 752 career tackles with 40 sacks and 12 interceptions.

Yeah, I Really Could Have Used Another Appendage.

On December 30, 2001, a Giants trick play, 86 Lambuth Special, failed with seven seconds left against the Eagles. At their own 20, the idea was for Kerry Collins to pass over the middle to Tiki Barber, who would cut right as Ron Dixon (who attended Lambuth in Tennessee) came up behind him, cutting left to accept a lateral.

The first segment worked beautifully. The seven-yard pass clicked, Dixon got the lateral and raced downfield. He made it 74 yards before being knocked out of bounds at the 6 by Damon Moore as time expired.

Linebacker Jesse Armstead was already annoyed that the Giants had surrendered 10 points in the last 1:49, and the final play exacerbated his anger. "I had no idea where Dixon was because I was so pissed off," he said. "I was so mad at how we came up short. If I had an extra leg, I'd be kicking myself."

For Armstead, being a Giant was an immense honor. On June 13, 2007, Armstead signed a one-day contract to officially retire as a Giant and in September 2008 was hired as a special assistant/consultant.

"In my blood, I always had New York Giants in it," Armstead said. "I went to Washington, another good organization, but there is no organization like the New York Giants. They always say the grass isn't greener on the other side; there is no grass outside New York. I never got over it. I played and I gave everything with the Redskins, but I knew my heart was in New York. I sometimes found myself getting myself in trouble because some of the guys with the Redskins would say something about the Giants. And I would defend the Giants. I had to realize, 'Hey, this is my team over here right now.' I would drive up to New York all of the time. [Linebacker] Antonio Pierce said, 'Why do you go to New York all of the time?' Because I love New York and I love the people."

Just before the Super Bowl, the Giants trampled the Vikings 41–0 in the title game, the biggest rout in NFC championship history. "That is one of the best moments right there outside of the Super Bowl," Armstead said. "A lot of people didn't give us a chance before that game started. The guys put up 41, and we kind of pulled back. There could have been 50-plus in that game."

Wide receiver Amani Toomer always remembered Armstead after his first practice when he was selected in the second round in 1996. "I thought I was doing pretty well. Then I got out there and ran a couple of routes," said Toomer. "I guess Jessie knocked the ball away from me. I didn't really think too much of it. He kind of gave me a little extra shove. I gave him a shove back. The next thing you know Jessie was in my face. I was like, 'This is a different league.' The thing that I remember about Jessie is his intensity—the way that he always prepared for a game. I never remember Jessie not being up for a game. No matter what the circumstances, he was prepared. I remember a lot about trying to practice against him. We definitely couldn't run any screens because he sniffed them out before we even tried to do them. I just remember him always coming to me and saying, 'You have to step it up, Toom, you have to step it up.' And I think he was one of the major reasons why I turned my career around. Come Sunday, No. 98 was ready to play."

Strahan had a slightly different perspective, having come into the league at the same time as Armstead. "I was fortunate enough to play a long time with Jessie," Strahan said. "Taste the pineapple, as we call it, go to Hawaii [for the Pro Bowl] with Jessie. Just to be on the field and go through so many tough experiences, tough games, tough seasons, great games, great seasons, Super Bowl. I had a chance to play with LT at the end of his career and some others—Michael Brooks and a lot of great players—but I never had a chance to play with a guy who was my peer, who came in with me that I just looked up to like him, because he never missed a game. And if he said it, he backed it up. He had the best football instinct I have ever been around. And you can tell that he loved what he did. Jessie is the best linebacker, the greatest linebacker that I have ever played with. I know I will never play with anybody quite like him. But just the leadership that Jessie displayed on the field, off the field, the way he carries himself even today, is something that should be admired not only by me, but by the younger guys. Jessie was not only an asset to the Giants but an asset to the NFL. And if we wouldn't have gotten screwed at the Super Bowl, he would have had a touchdown, and we would have won that game."

Sam Huff, No. 70

A dented helmet in the Hall of Fame. There is no better evidence of how Sam Huff played. The battered helmet is a lasting memento of the frigid 1962 NFL Championship Game and the singular battle between a rugged linebacker and a fearless back: Huff against Jim Taylor, the league's MVP.

"Jimmy Taylor was a romping, stomping fullback. It was a great rivalry because he...was not the type of back that would run out of bounds, he would try to run over you," Huff recalled in an interview a few years back when he was working as a broadcaster. "He used to say, 'I'll sting him, you know, when I get out in the open field, someone tries to tackle me, I'm going to sting him.' So you knew that when you played against him, you had to really tie that helmet on tight and tie your shoes on tight because he was a load. I mean, you just knew him, you get him out in the field and you get him one-on-one, you knew that he was going to turn on you and come at you like a Brahma bull. And you had to hit him with everything that you had."

And Robert E. Lee Samuel Huff, the son of a Morgantown coal-mining family who was selected in the third round of the draft in 1956, had plenty. He was an All-America guard at West Virginia, but once Giants defensive coordinator Tom Landry assessed Huff's vision of the field, speed, and tackling prowess, he was shifted to linebacker. Not just linebacker—middle linebacker—and the foundation of the first 4-3 defense, which was devised by Landry.

Landry had Jim Katcavage and Andy Robustelli on each end and Rosey Grier and Dick Modzelewski at tackles. The idea was for the ball carriers to be funneled to Huff or his outside mates, Harland Svare and Cliff Livingston. At 6'1", 230 pounds, Huff responded with aplomb and guts, anchoring the Giants defense through 1963 before he was traded to the Redskins.

Huff said that Cleveland's Jim Brown, with whom he also had immense collisions, was the best back he ever faced. But on December 30, 1962, with a 35 mph wind chilling Yankee Stadium below the stated 13 degrees, Huff had an epic war with Taylor in a game filled with magnificent athletes. Sixteen players from both teams eventually were enshrined in the Hall of Fame.

Legendary linebacker Sam Huff was the cornerstone of Tom Landry's 4-3 defense.
Photo courtesy of Getty Images

Taylor carried 31 times for 85 yards, some of the toughest of his career. "Did everything I could to that [expletive]," Huff said after the game, according to the book *The Magnificent Seven: The Championship Games That Built the Lombardi Dynasty.* Said Taylor, "I got my tongue split and my elbow sewed up at halftime. Sam Huff was a great line-backer, a Hall of Famer. We went after each other pretty good."

Packers guard and kicker Jerry Kramer, whose three field goals were the difference in the 16–7 Green Bay victory summed it up like this: "If

Seven Is Enough
In September 2004 lumbering, 317-pound lineman Fred "Big Dog" Robbins made his first career interception, and the Giants had six other turnovers. "It was a long time coming," he said. Then, feeling his oats, Robbins offered this basic assessment of winning in the NFL: "It is hard to lose when you get seven turnovers."

Taylor went up to get a program, Huff was supposed to hit him. Wherever Taylor went, Huff went with him. I remember sitting next to Jimmy on the way home, and he had his topcoat on. He never took it off. He had it over his shoulder, and the guy was shivering almost all the way home. He just got the [hell] beat out of him that day."

After Taylor scored the only Green Bay touchdown, a seven-yarder to provide a 10–0 lead in the second quarter, he barked back at Huff, who had mouthed off earlier. "He was saying 'You stink, Taylor,'" he said. "But when I scored, I said, 'How do I smell from here in the end zone?' A couple of times, at the bottom of the pile, the Giants were twisting my leg—anything to win. But that's okay—we wanted to win, too."

In his era, Huff recalled, "anything goes" was status quo. "We could do almost anything to receivers and backs," he said, "and even tackling them, when I first started, you could grab them by the nose guard and twist their head and pull them. Now you're not even allowed to make a tackle with your helmet. They fine you for helmet-to-helmet tackles. It's a different set of rules when we played in the '50s and '60s than these linebackers have today. I think it would be very difficult for me to play in today's game without being able to hit somebody with my helmet."

Huff, who played in six NFL title games and five Pro Bowls, didn't just pound running backs. He had 30 career interceptions. Above all, he loved being a Giant. When coach Allie Sherman traded him to Washington in 1964 as part of a veteran purge, he cried—and vowed revenge. Two years later, he sent the field-goal unit on without Redskins coach Otto Graham's approval—to rub salt in Sherman's wound in the closing seconds of a 72–41 massacre.

In 1959 Huff was the first NFL player to appear on the cover of *Time* magazine, and for a CBS News documentary narrated by Walter Cronkite, he was the first player to wear a microphone in practice and in an exhibition game. The program was called *The Violent World of Sam Huff.*

"I don't know whether I was truly violent or not, but when I put on that football uniform, I was a completely different person," Huff recalled. "As a matter of fact, when I played against my friends, I probably played harder and tougher against them than I did other people. I knocked my best friend—Joe Marconi who was playing for the Rams and who was my roommate at West Virginia for four years—I hit him in L.A. and knocked him clear over the bench. To me, I feel that you have to earn your friends' respect. And, if you quit, if you give up on them, they will not have the respect for you that they have for other linebackers. So that was always my belief. I never let up on anybody. I don't think I ever quit on a play. If you had the football, I was going to hit you, and when I hit you, I tried to hit you hard enough to hurt you. That's the way the game should be played."

Andy Robustelli: More than Robust

Can you spell long shot?

Andy Robustelli was happily playing sandlot football for a church league in Stamford, Connecticut, when a friend told him to go out for the team in his senior year of high school, where he starred in baseball and basketball.

Then Robustelli served in the Pacific in the U.S. Navy for two years during World War II before attending tiny Arnold College in nearby New Haven, where he played end on both sides of the ball and hit .400 as a third baseman/catcher. The Yankees wanted him to play in the Northern League.

In the meantime, Eddie Kotell, a Los Angeles Rams scout persuaded the club to draft Robustelli in the 19th round, and in 1951 he was offered a one-way ticket to training camp. "I was 25," Robustelli told the *Hartford Courant*. "I didn't want baseball because it might take a while to get to where I wanted to go. I was either going to make it with the Rams or not at training camp. I wanted that situation, to know immediately. Besides, if I didn't make it in the NFL, I'd probably be a physical education teacher."

Here's the lesson: it's never too late.

Robustelli not only made the Rams, he kicked off a Hall of Fame career in which he missed just one game in 14 years—and that was in 1951. With Elroy "Crazylegs" Hirsch and Tom Fears entrenched as wide receivers, Robustelli was inserted at defensive end, where his speed and strength on the pass rush helped carry the Rams to the NFL championship in his first of five years in Los Angeles. Opponents respected Robustelli, a quiet man who nonetheless was known as "the Enforcer" for his play on the field.

"In 1955, when I was with San Francisco, I was getting ready to throw for the winning TD," recalled Y.A. Tittle, who would be a Giant in 1961. "I cocked my arm. Andy suddenly ducked through, apparently from nowhere, grabbed the ball, and went in for the winning Rams TD." That was one of 22 fumble recoveries of his career.

But Stamford, the small city where he was raised by his father, Louis, a barber, and his mother, Katie, a seamstress, beckoned. His wife, Jean, was expecting their fourth child, and before the 1956 season, Robustelli asked if he could report late to camp.

The word spread that the durable Robustelli—who before the advent of game films was studying playbooks and reports constantly—was yearning to be back in the New York area. "We had heard that Andy wanted to come home," said Wellington Mara, then the Giants' general manager. "You bet I went after him." The Giants sent the Rams a future first-round draft choice, and it turned out to be one of the best deals the franchise ever made.

The Giants won the championship in 1956, destroying the Chicago Bears 47–7, and Robustelli played eight more seasons with the Giants, where his power and presence on the line with Jim Katcavage and tackles Roosevelt Grier and Dick Modzelewski formed the front of a defense that elicited the now-famous and oft-heard cheers of "Dee-fense!" from the faithful fans of New York not only in football, but in Knicks basketball as well.

Robustelli, the team's defensive captain for six years, was named league MVP in 1962, played in seven Pro Bowls—five as a Giant—and was named All-NFL seven times. He also played in eight championship

In the Lucky Zone

When players say they are totally zoned in on the field and anticipate plays, don't always believe them. Practice does help a bit, Michael Strahan said, after intercepting a pass in an exhibition game against the Carolina Panthers.

"Lucky goal-line play," Strahan confessed. "I have been covering [tight end Jeremy] Shockey in practice the last few weeks. He caught everything under the sun on me. I figured it's just another tight end, so I should catch the darn ball. I was able to catch it and make a play, and I should have just stayed in the end zone. I probably got a little rambunctious about how fast I was. To be honest, I didn't know exactly where I was."

games, two with the Rams and six with the Giants. He was elected to the Hall of Fame in 1971.

"I think what made Andy even better was going against [offensive tackle] Roosevelt Brown—two Hall of Famers," said Mara. "Practices often were better than the games."

After he retired in 1964, Robustelli was director of operations for the Giants for six years and owned a sporting goods store. It was that store that provided the 48 pairs of sneakers—and plenty of traction—for the Giants before the 1956 championship game.

Mara knew about the store, and Robustelli had new Keds sneakers that he felt would be ideal for a slippery, frozen field. Coach Jim Lee Howell had halfbacks Ed Hughes and Gene Filipski test the surface. Filipski made a few cuts with the sneakers. Hughes wore cleats and fell. "Everyone wears sneakers!" Howell barked.

Robustelli then founded Robustelli Corporate Services in Stamford, a firm that began as a travel agency and later expanded to specialize in travel packages for events such as Super Bowls, promotion, and media consulting. It was certainly a step up from his financial status as a player.

"I remember how we each got $2,800 as the winner's share in 1956 and how I had to go to work in my sports store in Stamford the very next day," he told the *Courant*. "You had to work in the off-season in those days, especially if you had a family like I did. The most money I ever made was $27,000, which I got for four straight years, from 1961 through 1964, when I was a player/coach."

Michael Strahan, Pete Townshend Wannabe?

To prepare for crowd noise in domed stadiums, the Giants, like many other teams, crank sound into the practice bubble. "As much as I hate it, it does help," Strahan said. "Especially for the communication-in-the-huddle standpoint. Because on the line pretty much everyone is going to watch the ball, I mean I don't think they can hear me, I can't hear myself a lot of times. But from the standpoint of being in the huddle and having to call plays and get personnel and everything, it gives everybody a little more practice at tuning in and listening real good." Strahan said the decibel level doesn't hurt his ears, "but there are times during practice when I would like to go over there and take a guitar or something and smash out all those speakers; live my rock 'n' roll fantasy out."

To be sure, Robustelli never forgot his roots. He was a neighbor and friend of the Valentine family in Stamford, and when their son, Bobby, was the fifth-overall selection in the June 1968 major league baseball draft, Robustelli was brought in to broker a deal with Dodgers general manager Al Campanis. Valentine got the contract, and years later became a successful major league manager with the Rangers and Mets.

Robustelli never would be confused with a slick, fast-talking agent. He preferred the idea of being in the background, a part of the big picture rather than preening for individual glory. "I spent years going around shaking a lot of hands and forcing myself to be someone that I'm really not," he said. "I never thought I did anything more. It was the team. We all were about winning. If I had my way, I would have had my teammates up there on the Hall of Fame stage with me."

Make no mistake, for all his humility, Robustelli earned the accolades. Ask Jim Brown, one of the top running backs of all time. "The two toughest men I ever knew," Brown said, "were Gino Marchetti [of the Baltimore Colts] and Andy Robustelli."

Emlen Tunnell: A Pro and a Pioneer

The word "pioneer" is all too often randomly tossed around. In the case of Emlen Tunnell, the term fits like an old glove. Not only was the Giants safety one of the best defensive backs ever, "Emlen the Gremlin," as he was known, was the first African American player in team history, the first full-time black assistant coach in the NFL, and the first African American inducted into the Hall of Fame.

Tunnell, who was born in 1925 outside of Philadelphia, was a three-sport athlete in high school, and, at 6'1", would eventually retire from the NFL in 1961 when he couldn't sprint, jump, and touch the crossbar between the goalposts. He had missed just four games in his 14-year NFL career and played in 158 consecutive games.

Gifted athletically, as a freshman tailback at the University of Toledo in Ohio, Tunnell broke his neck and had to wear a neck brace for a year, but then switched to basketball, and the Rockets reached the NIT finals.

When World War II began, Tunnell enlisted in the Coast Guard and, upon returning, attended the University of Iowa after a recommendation from former Hawkeyes tackle Jim Walker, whom he met while serving. "I knew blacks got a fair share there," he told reporters.

He was a quarterback in 1946, and a pass-catching fullback in 1947, when he became only the second Iowa player to catch three touchdown passes in a game. It was in Iowa that he began employing the basket-catch style later made popular by Giants center fielder Willie Mays.

But he left school in the summer of 1948, hitchhiked from Philadelphia to New York, and showed up unannounced at Giants offices seeking a tryout. Based on his numbers in Iowa, he was given one and then offered a one-year contract.

He preferred offense but that fall intercepted four passes in a game against the Packers and became a prolific defender at the top of the Giants' 6-1-4 "umbrella defense"—the predecessor to the "nickel," in which two defensive ends dropped back into short pass coverage.

"Emlen changed the theory of defensive safeties," Giants coach Jim Lee Howell told the *New York Times*. "He would have been too big for the job earlier, and they'd have made him a lineman. But he had such strength, such speed, and such quickness I'm convinced he was the best safety ever to play."

His 79 career interceptions led the league until 1979, when Paul Krause finished with 81. He remains No. 2 on the all-time list. Rod Woodson broke Tunnell's record for career interception return yardage (1,483). "At first I thought he was lucky," Frank Gifford once said, "then I realized he was great."

Giants fans called Tunnell "offense on defense." In the Giants' home opener on October 14, 1951, he returned four kicks for 178 yards and a touchdown in a 28–17 win.

In 1952 he gained more yards on punt and kickoff returns and interceptions (924) than the NFL's rushing leader, Dan Towler of the L.A. Rams, who registered 894. In 1953 he was second on the Giants in offensive yards.

In 11 years with the Giants, Tunnell was named All-NFL four times and played in nine Pro Bowls. He ended his career with nearly 1,300 interception return yards and 2,209 yards gained returning punts, some of which came when he joined the Packers in 1959.

As more African Americans came into the league, Tunnell was praised for helping the transition. "One of the reasons we never had problems was because of Em Tunnell," Giants operations director Andy Robustelli told the *New York Times*. "Emlen was good to all people. He was a hell of a decent person who meant a lot to young ballplayers."

Tunnell went to Green Bay in 1959 after 11 seasons in New York to be reunited with former Giants coordinator Vince Lombardi, then the head coach of the Packers, as a player/coach. Lombardi said Tunnell "meant a lot to the Packers then. He was a pastor, a cheerleader, and a coach as well as a player."

William Joseph, Comedian

The public and the press certainly can have misconceptions about a player's personality. Take lineman William Joseph, for instance. "Everybody thinks that he is this big, quiet teddy bear," said Michael Strahan. "William is a comedian. And as we say, 'He's one of the biggest haters on the D-line.' But William is a lot of fun to be around and he is generally a good guy. He works hard. You watch film and he is running down the field the other day after a receiver. Every other D-lineman was basically still at the line.... William understands exactly what his role is, he seems to be more comfortable. Just listening to he and Osi [Umenyiora] talk to each other, they challenge each other, because they both came in at the same time; one wants to outdo the other. Osi says, 'You are a first-round bust.' William says: 'You are a second-round bust.' So they stay on each other and make sure they both go out there and play well."

One of his acolytes was Herb Adderley, the Packers' first-round draft choice in 1961. A halfback at Michigan State, Adderley was moved to flanker during his rookie year and returned kickoffs, but the 22-year-old seemed to lack some spark.

Lombardi asked Tunnell to speak with Adderley, and Tunnell told him that the youngster wanted to play defensive back. On Thanksgiving Day in 1961 against the Detroit Lions, with less than a week of practice, Adderley replaced the injured Hank Gremminger in the third quarter. Minutes later, Adderley intercepted Jim Ninowski to set up a touchdown that proved to be the game-deciding score. Adderley was the Packers' left cornerback for nine years, intercepted 39 passes, and returned a team-record seven for touchdowns.

After the Packers whipped the Giants 37–0 in the 1961 NFL Championship Game, Tunnell retired but began scouting. He signed on full-time with the Giants in 1963. He later became an assistant coach, and long before all the lobbying and the NFL's attempts to develop African American head coaches, Tunnell argued that blacks deserved a chance to do the job. Unfortunately, he never had the opportunity to break that color barrier. Tunnell died of a heart attack at the Giants' practice facility in Pleasantville, New York, in July 1975. He was 50. His passing ended a too-short, but fruitful professional career that started when he hitchhiked to the Giants' offices for that tryout.

When Dick McCann, the curator of the Hall of Fame in 1967, called Tunnell to notify him of his selection, Tunnell asked: "Who should I thank?" Said McCann, "Thank yourself."

The Crunch Bunch:
Van Pelt, Kelley, Carson, and Taylor

On September 30, 2007, in an incredible display of pass-rushing, the Giants sacked Eagles quarterback Donovan McNabb a dozen times— tying an NFL record—in front of a sellout crowd at Giants Stadium and four honorary captains.

Watching from the sideline was the quartet of legendary linebackers from the 1970s and '80s: Hall of Famers Lawrence Taylor and Harry

Carson, and Brad Van Pelt and Brian Kelley. "We take credit for it," Carson said after the game. "It was the 'Crunch Bunch.' They saw us there."

Three of those sacks were by Mathias Kiwanuka, a Boston College grad in his second pro season whose grandfather had been prime minister of Uganda. "If seeing those guys on the sideline doesn't inspire you," Kiwanuka said, "I don't think you need to be in this league because those are some of the greatest to ever play this game and wear these uniforms."

Veteran end Michael Strahan and the new kids on the block— Kiwanuka, Osi Umenyiora, and Justin Tuck—were dubbed the "Sack Pack," but they clearly had much more to accomplish. After Strahan tackled McNabb for a three-yard loss in the second quarter to break a tie with Taylor and raise his total to 133.5 sacks in a 15-year career with the Giants, Taylor was the typical competitive LT: "I want to congratulate Michael on setting the new official career sack record for the Giants," he said. "And I want to remind him that I had 9.5 sacks [as a rookie in 1981] before they even started counting them, so he has some more work to do."

If nothing else, the Crunch Bunch was known for its hard-hitting ensemble approach. Although rooted in the late 1970s, the foursome was the bright spot from 1981—when a 9–7 record vaulted the Giants to the NFL playoffs for the first time in 18 years—through 1982 and 1983, when the team was 7–17–1, although the defense allowed an average of just 17.8 points per game in the first of those two seasons.

"I feel as comfortable with them as I do with my brothers," Van Pelt, the strong-side linebacker and Michigan State multisport star who was voted the Giants Player of Decade in the 1970s, said in 2004. "Obviously, your brothers are your brothers. But these three are probably the closest thing to them. Brian and I played 11 years together. I played nine with Harry. Lawrence being the guy [he is], it didn't take long for him to fit right in and become one of the guys. I can't really explain why, but they're the only three [players] I stay close with."

Van Pelt and Kelley, both drafted in 1973, were the elder statesmen of the Crunch Bunch, a battering-ram unit that was christened before the 1982 season. To promote the name and earn some pocket money, the players incorporated a company called "The Board of De-wreckers" specifically to sell a $5 poster featuring them in uniform, wearing blue hard hats and glowering from a John Deere bulldozer on a construction site. Today those posters are worth hundreds more, and to some fans the memories are priceless.

Carson was drafted in 1976, and in the next five seasons, Van Pelt made five Pro Bowls and Carson two. When Taylor roared aboard in 1981 from North Carolina, Kelley moved to inside linebacker.

After the 1983 season, coach Bill Parcells was retooling the team and traded Kelley and Van Pelt. They were replaced by inside backer Gary Reasons and Byron Hunt on the outside, who would help the franchise win its first Super Bowl in 1987.

The Crunch Bunch had been broken up, but only on the field. Their bonds would last far longer. "I've known Brad for 31 years, Harry for 28, and LT for 23 years," Kelley said in 2005. "How do you explain those relationships? We have the same relationship off the field we had on the field. We had the trust of each other. When I was on the field, I knew Brad wasn't going to let the tight end come off and hit me. When you have trust like that on the field—it's the same with LT and Harry— I think it just evolves off the field. We trust each other that we're not going to take advantage of each other, that we're not going to take advantage of LT's fame. He knows that he has three friends that he can call when he wants to speak to someone."

Said Carson: "We were considered, during our time, probably the best group of linebackers in the league. We didn't win—as we did in '86.

Mum's the Word on No. 98

In 1980 George Young was scouting the North Carolina–Clemson game and was slackjawed about Lawrence Taylor's performance. Not only did he avoid speaking to other general managers and scouts about it, his lips were sealed.

"I've never seen a guy dominate a game like that," the Giants' former general manager said. "I came back to New York, and someone asked me if I thought Hugh Green [of Pittsburgh] was the best linebacker in the country. I said, 'Uh-uh.' He asked who was, and I said, 'I'm not telling.'"

After the New Orleans Saints drafted running back George Rogers first overall in the draft, Young took No. 98, changed his number to 56, and also changed the direction of the franchise that had foundered for 18 seasons.

We did that with Carl [Banks], Gary Reasons, Lawrence, and I. With that group we have a different kind of relationship." With the Crunch Bunch, he said, "when we go somewhere together, I think what happens is we assume the roles that we had when we played. We are four guys who genuinely like one another. We went through a lot of good stuff together; we went through some bad stuff together.... It is sort of like a brotherhood."

Brad Van Pelt

Brad Van Pelt stood out wherever he went. He was the all-American kid—blond, buffed, strong-jawed, the son of an NFL quarterback. In high school, Van Pelt excelled in three sports. He turned down contracts from the California Angels and Detroit Tigers before attending MSU. A right-handed pitcher, Van Pelt then helped the Spartans win the Big Ten Conference championship in 1971. Van Pelt—also a power forward on the MSU varsity hoops squad—won seven varsity letters and was coveted by baseball teams before the Giants picked him in the second round in 1973. Giants co-owner Wellington Mara outbid baseball's St. Louis Cardinals.

"I have only two regrets in life, and one of them is that I wished I would have waited to sign my first pro contract with the Giants," he once said. "Because of that, I had to forgo my last seasons in basketball and baseball. I would've loved to play those last seasons and earn nine letters."

As a safety in college, Van Pelt won the Maxwell Award as college football's best player—the first time ever by a defensive player. At State, he wore No. 10, and asked for that number with the Giants. Linebackers, according to NFL rules at the time, were assigned numbers between 50 and 59. The club found a loophole: they listed Van Pelt as a backup kicker, which he was in college. "It helped my career. I started to get to be a better linebacker and I started getting noticed a little more— that number, they couldn't forget it," he once recalled. "Ten just doesn't belong out there on defense. It was a lucky number for me. I was very fortunate the Giants allowed me to have it."

In his rookie year, Kelley remembered, the Giants were loaded at line-backer and tried the 6'5", 235-pound Van Pelt at tight end, but he didn't fit in. A groin strain also limited his playing time. A year later, head coach Bill Arnsparger and linebackers coach Marty Schottenheimer "put him in front of a tight end and that was history after that," Kelley said.

With his size and speed, Van Pelt chased down quarterbacks like the Cowboys' Danny White and was a blanket in pass coverage. In 14 seasons in the NFL—11 with the Giants—Van Pelt played in 184 regular-season games and had 20 interceptions, 14 fumble recoveries, and an unofficial sack total of 24.5.

When the Giants, looking to get younger, drafted another talented MSU linebacker, Carl Banks, Van Pelt was traded to the Vikings for running back Tony Galbreath. But he didn't report and hooked on with the Raiders for a year and then the Browns in 1986.

The years that Van Pelt played not only were some of the worst in Giants history, they were also when the team kept moving around. He was one of the few players who suited up in Yankee Stadium, the Yale Bowl, Shea Stadium, and Giants Stadium. In only one of his 11 seasons, 1981, did the team have a winning record.

Van Pelt returned to Michigan to complete his education and kept in regular touch with the Crunch Bunch, attending events, charity golf tournaments, Pro Bowls in Hawaii, and occasional Giants games. He and Kelley, who marvelled at Van Pelt's disdain for material things, spoke regularly by phone and stayed in contact with Carson and Taylor, all of whom had been divorced.

Carson remembered Van Pelt's generosity. "I had a couple of golf tournaments down in Carolina, and he didn't hesitate in coming down to participate because it was me, and the relationship was special," he said. "Brad was very meticulous in signing autographs. We would be signing as a group, and he would have to be the last one in line because he would hold everybody up because he wrote his autograph in such a way that everybody could understand it and he didn't rush through it."

In October 2004 Carson assembled the Crunch Bunch as part of a daylong Habitat for Humanity project with former president Jimmy Carter to pour cement and build walls for 150 houses in Puebla, Mexico. On the day they arrived, Van Pelt was being kidded because he brought his own tool belt; Taylor arrived in black golf slacks, a white shirt, and a black vest, which he described as his "work clothes."

"You see Jimmy Carter up there laying bricks with everyone else," Van Pelt said at the time. "It was the first time I ever met a president. It was quite an experience.... I was disappointed that we were heading back so soon. A couple more days would have been fun."

The calls and the far-flung camaraderie continued until February 17, 2009, when a phone call came that no one wanted to hear. Van Pelt's fiancée relayed the news that he had died of a heart attack at home in Michigan at age 57.

"It was total devastation," Kelley told reporters. "I've known him longer than my wife and my kids. Football was 11 years of our life. We had 25 other years when we were together, did things together, and still are doing them together, us and LT and Harry Carson. It's sort of like losing a limb because the four of us are so close."

Brian Kelley

Unlike Van Pelt, Brian Kelley's geographic route to New Jersey for his role in the Crunch Bunch was far longer. Kelley was raised in California and played linebacker at California Lutheran, where his 16 career interceptions were a school record. In 1972 he was the most valuable player of the NAIA national championship game.

All that stability went awry when he was drafted by the Giants in the 14th round in 1973, the start of a bleak period that many call "the Wilderness Years" of the storied franchise. In Kelley's 11 years, the Giants record was a dismal 49–108–1.

For Kelley, the timing couldn't have been worse. At the beginning of his career, the Giants were stumbling badly; at the end, they were on the upswing, and would win a Super Bowl two years after he left.

"We went through five head coaches and we must have gone through 30 assistant coaches. It was like one of those swinging barroom doors," Kelley told Giants.com. "People were coming and going left and right. And I think it was '74, we had the strike that lasted, which set us back again. I think we had about 200 people in camp at one time. There was a lot I wasn't used to."

Kelley led the team in tackles from 1974 through 1976, but he said he was lucky to have played as a rookie. There were already five linebackers in camp—Jim Files, Pat Hughes, John Douglas, Ron Hornsby, and Henry Reed—and Van Pelt was their first pick.

He essentially made the club as a quality special-teamer and started only due to injuries. Van Pelt was sidelined and in the last preseason game, Kelley recalled, "Hughes sprained his ankle real bad. Basically, there was nobody to play except me at weak-side linebacker. That was a shocker. We played in Cleveland, and I was in the dugout when they announced my name as the starting right outside backer. I just went 'Oh, my God.' I was quite fortunate. It was unfortunate for some guys. Once I got the opportunity, I was able to produce."

Unfortunately, the Giants offense didn't. The quarterback carousel spun: Jerry Golsteyn, Jim Del Gaizo, Scott Brunner, Craig Morton, Joe Pisarcik. Kelley said he couldn't even remember them all. "We almost had a different quarterback every year," he said.

On defense, Kelley—who wasn't the fastest linebacker but was bright—called the signals. In 1981, Taylor's first season, Kelley was credited with 186 tackles, including 106 solo takedowns. Like Van Pelt, who was let go after Banks was acquired, Kelley was traded to the Chargers in 1984 when Reasons arrived.

"I'm happy with what I did," Kelley once said. "I'm never satisfied. I would have loved to have been able to go to a Super Bowl and win a Super Bowl ring and stay on another two or three years with the Giants."

Kelley never stayed out West, though. He had returned to New Jersey in 1980 after spending the offseasons in California and, after retiring, stayed in the Garden State and became a financial advisor whose clients include current players.

"A lot of people play a lot of years and they never make it to the Super Bowl," Kelley lamented. "Then you have guys that ride the bench for one or two years and they win two Super Bowl rings."

Lawrence Taylor
The youngest member of the Crunch Bunch, Lawrence Taylor, never rode the bench. Yet he has two Super Bowl rings. And a ton of other hardware.

The 6'3", 237-pound linebacker—now widely considered the top linebacker in NFL history—was selected No. 2 overall behind George Rogers in the 1981 draft. Giants general manager George Young didn't mince words on the North Carolina star. "Taylor is the best college linebacker I've ever seen," he said. "Sure, I saw Dick Butkus play. There's no doubt in my mind about Taylor. He's bigger and stronger than Butkus was. On the blitz, he's devastating."

As a rookie in 1981, Taylor set the tone for his pro career. He racked up 133 tackles, 9.5 sacks, eight passes defended, two forced fumbles, a fumble recovery, and an interception. In 1982 and 1983 he would add another 16.5 sacks, as he changed the outside linebacker position forever with speed, recklessness, intensity, and muscle.

Taylor would be named Defensive Rookie of the Year and the overall Defensive Player of the Year by the Associated Press in 1981 and made the Pro Bowl 10 times in a career that was dotted with contract disputes and ravaged by alcohol and drug abuse, which Taylor—by then known as LT—publicly recalled in graphic detail in his autobiographies and in television interviews. He admitted to cocaine abuse in 1985 and called golf his "detox tank," but was suspended for 30 days in 1988 for failing a drug test. He relapsed again in the '90s, rehabilitated himself, and has since gained more control of his life, appearing in movies and on the hit television show *Dancing with the Stars* in 2009.

His Crunch Bunch experience, however, was in his formative years in the NFL, although the signs of his greatness and wild side were becoming evident. For example, he chose No. 56, he said, because he was inspired by Thomas "Hollywood" Henderson of the Dallas Cowboys, who would hardly be described as a traditional role model. The flamboyant Henderson, as it was discovered later, used cocaine on the sideline during games, and after being dumped by the Cowboys, served two years in prison. Henderson cleaned up his life afterward, and in a bizarre twist, won $28 million in the Texas lottery.

"On the pass rush, he's an animal," quarterback Phil Simms said of Taylor at the time. "He's either going to run around you or over you. With his quickness, he's full speed after two steps." In his first NFL exhibition game on August 8, 1981, Taylor had two sacks in the Giants' 23–7 defeat of the Chicago Bears.

Lawrence Taylor revolutionized the linebacker position during his 13-year Giants career. Photo courtesy of Getty Images

Taylor's presence immediately improved the Giants, who rose from 4–12 in 1980 to 9–7 and a wild-card playoff spot. In that postseason, the Giants upset the Eagles 27–21 for their first playoff victory since 1958.

"One of LT's single most amazing games was the playoff game in '81 against Philadelphia," former defensive coach Bill Belichick said, "because he not only dominated on defense, but also dominated on special teams, forcing two fumbles by Wally Henry."

The Giants built a 20–0 lead and hung on. Scott Brunner threw touchdown passes to Leon Bright, John Mistler, and Tom Mullady, and Mark Haynes recovered a fumble in the end zone. But they would advance no further. The eventual Super Bowl–champion 49ers won the next weekend, 38–24, one of the first times that a team assigned an offensive lineman, John Ayers, a guard, specifically to block Taylor.

Even in the strike-shortened 1982 season, Taylor's reputation grew during the nationally televised Thanksgiving Day game against the Detroit Lions. With the score tied at 6 early in the fourth quarter, Lions quarterback Gary Danielson tossed a pass toward the left sideline. Taylor read the play and reacted, intercepting the ball and streaking 97 yards for a back-breaking, dramatic touchdown and a 13–6 win.

In 1983 coach Bill Parcells was elevated to head coach, and Taylor missed some of training camp in a contract holdout. He would have nine sacks, but the team finished 3–12–1, prompting a Parcells purge.

Taylor and Carson would receive plenty of help from Simms, running back Joe Morris, tight end Mark Bavaro, and others in their next seasons, including during the unforgettable Super Bowl run in 1986. Taylor would continue to battle his demons and be part of another Super Bowl victory in 1991, but his performances sagged in the next few years, and he finally retired, crying on the sideline after a 49ers playoff rout on January 15, 1994.

His high-profile, celebrity status allowed him to work as a football analyst for TNT, partake in Wrestlemania, and test the waters as an actor. His on-field excellence brought him to the Hall of Fame, elected on the first ballot in 1999.

The ties to the Crunch Bunch remained.

"I think it sort of goes back to football the way it used to be," Carson said. "Playing for one another and having a tremendous sense of pride in our unit as a group. I think it is well documented that before Lawrence got there, we felt pretty good within ourselves that we were a good group of linebackers. Then when Lawrence got there, we all saw his talent, and he just made us even better than what we thought we could be.... I would venture to say at one point, we were probably the best linebacking corps in the NFL. That is something that doesn't fade overnight or through the years."

On that one-day trip to Mexico with Habitat for Humanity, according to Carson, he saw a changed Taylor. "He volunteered for the heavy, dirty part of the job," Carson said after returning. "The same work ethic Lawrence had on the field, he exhibited it in building that house. It is a different side of Lawrence that very few people have gotten an opportunity to see.... I was very proud of him. I think he may have learned a little something different about himself through the experience. Often times, we take what we have for granted. And all of a sudden you find yourself in a situation where you are working side by side with someone who has a house that is like one-fifth the size of your house and they are so appreciative. And they are moving into a place with running water, someplace with a toilet, with lights. So I think he probably is counting his blessings and feels a little bit more thankful for what he has now."

Harry Carson

In Harry Carson's case, he never forgot his past. He grew up as the youngest of six children of a railroad worker in Florence, South Carolina, a farming area during the Civil War that has been transformed into a bustling medical-research center.

As a youngster, Carson recalled quitting the local football team after the first day of drills. "It was a shock to my system," he said. "But I did not like the taste of being a quitter. The next day I went to the Florence Boys' Club and I joined the team. I had an opportunity to play and ease back into what football is all about."

In high school, where he was senior class president, cochairman of the school's Bi-Racial Committee and ROTC Commander, Carson earned a scholarship to South Carolina State, a small black school in Orangeburg, and never missed a game at defensive end for the Bulldogs. He lasted until the fourth round of the 1976 draft and was selected by the Giants. Schottenheimer, as he had with Van Pelt, turned him into a linebacker, and Carson was named to the All-Rookie team.

Carson would initially play inside linebacker in the 3-4 with the Crunch Bunch and then anchor the middle in the 4-3 afterward. That was his milieu. He was an emotional captain of the Giants for 10 of his 13 years and "quarterback" and spiritual leader of the defense.

"I still remember, and I will remember this for the rest of my life, the Super Bowl against Denver [in 1987]," he told Peter King of *Sports Illustrated*. "We had three captains—me, Phil Simms, and George Martin. But when it came time for the coin toss before the game, I started to go out and looked around for those guys. Bill Parcells said to me: 'No. You go. Just you.' And that was about the coolest feeling I've ever had in the world—going out to midfield for the Super Bowl, as the lone captain. There were nine Denver Broncos out there, and me. Just me. An awesome responsibility. The greatest respect."

Without question, he was the Giants' run-stuffer, meeting backs head on, shoulder-to-shoulder, helmet-to-helmet. He led the Giants defenders in tackles five seasons and was named to the Pro Bowl nine times.

No wonder that Belichick, former Giants defensive coordinator and head coach of the Super Bowl champion New England Patriots, considers Carson the best all-around linebacker he ever coached.

In one astounding performance against the Green Bay Packers in 1982, he had 20 solo tackles and five assists. On December 7, 1986, as the Giants stormed to their first Super Bowl, he registered 12 solo tackles and intercepted a pass against the Washington Redskins that assured the Giants of the NFC East title. And in the first-half goal-line stand in the Super Bowl against the Broncos, Carson nailed Denver back Gerald Willhite for no gain in what many considered one of the crucial plays of the game.

From 1981 to 1987, with Carson at the core of the defense, the Giants averaged 3.59 yards per opponents' rushing attempt, one of the lowest in the modern era.

But the week-after-week pounding, the bone-jarring contact, left its mark. Carson suffered from headaches, dizziness, blurred vision, and depression, all residue of concussions of varying degrees. He estimated that he sustained between 15 and 20 concussions since college. He never mentioned the symptoms, hiding behind the stereotype of the invincible football player, and kept playing. The problems, including forgetfulness, continued when he retired after the 1988 season and initially went into broadcasting, a field he had broached in his last two seasons in New York with a gig at WCBS-TV (channel 2).

With his knowledge of the game, he received plenty of offers—he cohosted CNN's *NFL Preview*, was a studio analyst for MSG Network, and reported for ABC's *Good Morning America*. His concern and anxiety mounted, however, when his post-concussion syndrome prevented him from assuredly remembering names and statistics, and in 1990 he told a doctor about the symptoms. In the ensuing years he learned to cope with the limitations and has become a successful businessman, spokesman, and a board member for organizations researching brain-trauma injuries and dozens of charities.

When he realized that former NFL players were suffering from similar problems and other medical issues and the league wasn't providing enough in diagnosis and care, Carson took up that cause as well and has made significant strides.

For several years, his nominations for the Hall of Fame were rejected, and after missing out, he become so disenchanted with the process that in 2004, he asked Hall executives to remove his name from consideration. That request was denied, and in 2006 he was voted into Canton. Carson used the public forum of what he and many others considered a long-overdue induction to call out the league for its insufficient programs and benefits for retired players and its lack of integration in coaching. "I would hope that the leaders of the NFL, the commissioner, and the players association do a much better job of looking out for those individuals," Carson said from the podium. "You got to look out for 'em. If we made the league what it is, you have to take better care of your own.... I hope that the owners and those in the positions of power will open it up to a greater sense of diversity."

Jeff Nixon, a former free safety for the Buffalo Bills and a leader in the effort to increase retirement benefits for retired players, applauded Carson's stance. "You will always be remembered for the courage it took to be the first to speak out on these issues at the HOF Induction Ceremony," Nixon wrote in a letter to Carson and distributed to the media. "It was not the politically correct thing to do, but it was the right thing to do…and it has inspired many more to join in the efforts to help the retired players that worked so hard to make the NFL and the NFLPA what they are today."

That was just the opening of the speech. Once Carson made his point, he revealed much more about himself and his perspective on his role in life, remarks that deserve to be excerpted and remembered for the portrait of a notable athlete and man, a true Giant:

I am the one individual who probably should not be standing before you this afternoon. I am so much unlike a football player. Physically, I look like a football player, but inside I have my mother's heart. My mother's heart is being gentle, being caring, looking out for people.

I realized that by having that opportunity to play in the National Football League, it wasn't just about dollars, it wasn't about cars or anything like that, it was much greater. For me, it was about having the opportunity. Let me just tell you, when I played on any level, there had been players much better than me, much better. When I used to play sandlot ball, I wasn't the first one picked. When I played high school ball, I wasn't the best. When I played college ball, I wasn't the best my first two years. My last two years, I was pretty damn good.

For whatever reason, I think God chose me. I'm not a religious person, but I am a spiritual person. God chose me to do something that was very special. When I stand here before you today…this is not about me, this is about my family, this is about Gladys Carson, who took my name and put it on the altar every Sunday. It wasn't about me being a football player, it was about me being a man and staying out of trouble. It was about Florence, South Carolina. It was about my friends who I played with.…

I've done the best that I could. I'm here maybe a little late, but I'm here. I don't care how long it's taken. All of you who have been my supporters, you Giant fans, you know what it's all about, you know what it's all about. You've been there for me. You remember those years when the Giants sucked, the Giants were awful. You know about it. Even the Redskin fans know about it. Even the Cowboy fans know about it. Even the Eagles fans know about it.

I'm excited about being that person to be able to represent any football player who snapped on that chin strap, any football player who has had a sprained ankle, any football player who knows what it's like to not want to have to run an extra lap, an extra sprint, but he does it.

I think the most important thing about being here today, seeing this bust, I come from a very proud race of people. When I think about those who proceeded me who never had this opportunity. We didn't come through Ellis Island. I think about all of those, my ancestors who never could even dream about a moment like this.... As I said before, I'm not a religious person, but I'm a spiritual person, I feel very strongly that my maker put me in this position for a reason, and that is to represent all of those who preceded me and to represent those who will come after me.

I'm told that this bust will be around for a good 40,000 years. That's a long time. I'm looking at my granddaughter here, my nieces, my granddaughter's children and grandchildren...to be able to come to Canton, Ohio, to see what their ancestor did and to know there's absolutely nothing beyond their reach.

chapter 8

Royalty in Football and Family

Tim Mara

Tim Mara liked sure things. As a legal bookmaker in New York in 1925, he knew the odds. On August 1, 1925, Mara was at a meeting angling to invest in boxer Gene Tunney, which seemed like a sure thing. Instead, he wound up with an opportunity to purchase the All-Collegian Professional Football Club Inc., the New York franchise in the nascent National Professional Football League.

Mara was wary but gambled. He forked over the $500 fee, which, he discovered, got him nothing but paper rights: no players, no coach, no field, no equipment. Mara persuaded several friends to buy shares in the new corporation and decided to rent the Polo Grounds. The club was named after the baseball team already playing in the ballpark in upper Harlem, the Giants.

What Mara didn't realize at the time was that the real asset in the future of the New York football Giants—the devoted soul of a franchise who would be immensely influential in the growth of the National Football League—wasn't part of the deal. It was his youngest son, Wellington, who was nine years old.

Tim Mara scrambled on the business side, trying to sell or give away tickets and generate interest in the newspapers in the team's October 18 home opener against the Frankford Yellow Jackets after they had lost the first two games of the season. Of the 25,000 who attended, about half were there for free.

Giants owner Tim Mara founded the franchise in 1925. Photo courtesy of Getty Images

Seventeen-year-old Jack Mara, Tim's elder son, handled a sideline yard-marker; Wellington sat on the bench with his father. One of the club's prized signings, partly for promotional purposes, was halfback Jim Thorpe, who was broken down from injuries and alcohol at age 37. Thorpe's injured left leg didn't allow him to even finish the first half, and he would never play for the Giants again.

On the sideline, ballboy Wellington Mara caught a cold, and Mara's wife was annoyed. She noticed that the Giants bench, on the south side of the field, was in the shade; the visitors' remained in the sun. "She told Pop to switch the benches," Wellington Mara once recalled. "It was either that or leave me home, so Pop switched benches. And they've stayed switched ever since."

That was indeed the case later at Yankee Stadium; at Giants Stadium in East Rutherford in New Jersey, which began hosting games in 1976; and would be for the new billion-dollar stadium under construction in 2009. Family first.

The Fourth Cut Is the Roughest

When coaches use language from other sports to describe traits or the progress of players, it can be quite descriptive—and amusingly understandable.

Here's tight ends coach Mike Pope responding to questions about Vishante Shiancoe: "He practices when he's banged up a little bit. He's a tough guy, but he has a long way to go. Because he is coming out of a smaller program with not a lot of exposure to major-college football, I think he still has a long way to go. You knew he was a diamond in the rough, your accent on the rough. You know how golf is: first cut, second cut, third cut, fourth cut. Well, he was fourth cut."

Jim Fassel also used similar imagery when discussing the fumble-prone Tiki Barber, and how to cure it. "Sometimes I think what happens is, whether you're a running back carrying the ball or you're a free-throw shooter or a golfer or whatever, sometimes you get a little bit out of technique and you need someone to tell you," Fassel said. "Tiger Woods has a guy telling him—and he is the greatest golfer in the history of whatever—and he still has a guy watch his swing and see if he is a little out; that is the kind of thing you notice, maybe he is starting to do that now—we need to make sure he gets back in place."

Some executives will use the baseball analogy. When the Giants selected Mathias Kiwanuka, a defensive end from Boston College in the 2006 draft, general manager Ernie Accorsi sounded like a major league manager: "It is my philosophy and is shared by the people in our organization, you never, never have enough pass rushers. And he is a pass rusher.... And I know that he is at a position where we have two Pro Bowlers, but there are different ways to use pass rushers. And like home-run hitters and pitchers, you just never have enough of them, because we have other needs, too. But when you put pressure on the passer, everybody else's job is easier."

Wellington Mara

Wellington dove headlong into the family's new occupation. He not only watched games from the bench, he shot some of the first game films with a movie camera. At practices, he shined shoes and ran errands.

In 1930 Tim Mara divided his ownership interests between Jack and Wellington, who was 14 and becoming consumed with players and statistics. Four years before the first NFL Draft, he put together a list of the top pro prospects in college. There were no fantasy leagues or computers back then, of course. At that point, he was just 16 and attending Loyola High School.

During one summer as a teenager, Wellington's mother allowed him to live with the team in training camp, and the players who had christened him "the Duke" employed him during practice. He was assigned to place balls next to center Mel Hein, who was snapping them for kicks. At one point, Hein, blocking an invisible opponent, lunged forward and accidently caught Mara with an elbow in the face, knocking him down and blackening an eye. When his mother picked up the newspapers the next day, this headline was not what she wanted to read over breakfast: "Young Mara First Casualty of Giant Camp."

"If Pop hadn't talked Mother out of it, I'd have been home that afternoon," Mara recalled. "There was so much commotion, the other players started kidding Mel he'd lose his job."

While at Fordham University, Mara scouted college players. He signed Alphonse "Tuffy" Leemans after watching him play at George Washington University; he was the second player drafted by the Giants in 1936. Leemans would lead the NFL in rushing with 830 yards, and in 1941 led the team in both passing and rushing.

He also met Vince Lombardi at Fordham, and their relationship led to Lombardi mentoring the Giants offense for five years in the glory years, from 1954 to 1958, before becoming the legendary coach at Green Bay.

After graduating from Fordham in 1937, Wellington moved to the front office, and while Jack handled the business side, he preferred to be a hands-on personnel director: making football decisions; continuing to attend training camp, daily practices, and games; taking notes; circling the field; speaking to coaches and players. The only time he was not

Old Soldiers Never Retire

The thrill of competition is a powerful tonic. When Bill Parcells returned to NFL coaching, Ernie Accorsi explained why he thought certain coaches never really retire. "It never surprises me," Accorsi said. "There are so few who don't come back. I was trying to think other than [Ara] Parseghian, I mean Bear Bryant died, but they all come back. Everett Williams had a great line, 'Once you've been exposed to contest living, it is tough not to have contest living.' Competition every day—he was a trial lawyer."

closely involved with the team was when he served as a lieutenant commander in the Navy during World War II in both the Atlantic and Pacific.

Even as a team vice president, when he moved to the upstairs press box, he would use a Polaroid to snap pictures of opponents' game formations and lower them to the bench in a weighted sock.

And Mara was terrific in that role, personally drafting Frank Gifford, Kyle Rote, and Roosevelt Grier. In trades, he acquired players such as Y.A. Tittle, Andy Robustelli, Del Shofner, Pat Summerall, Joe Walton, Dick Lynch, Harland Svare, and Erich Barnes.

Even in his later years, Mara was a wise presence in the Giants' war room on draft days. "The scouts were the people he loved the most," recalled Ernie Accorsi, a former general manager of the Colts and Browns who was the Giants' general manager from 1998 to 2006. "He said it was his favorite time of the year. He was sicker at the time than we realized, but he was here for all of the draft meetings. He would sit in the back room with his notebook and follow every line of the draft. He just absolutely loved it."

Accorsi, a savvy fellow himself who'd drafted John Elway and engineered a draft-day swap with San Diego for Eli Manning, said Mara would discuss every pick outside the room with the head coach, John Mara, and co-owner Bob Tisch, who, like Wellington, died in 2005.

"The great thing about Mr. Mara was that he influenced so much late in the draft," said Accorsi. "He would come up to the board and remind us—'You guys said that this guy would be a great guy to look at in the sixth round and you don't have him up on the board now. Don't forget him.' I won't tell you the player, but I remember him doing it in the seventh round, and we ended up picking the player. We kind of had lost sight of the player in the seventh round. He watched, he had his Buschbaum [scouting] book out and he had our records and he would sit there line by line and never leave the room. He would eat his lunch there."

Accorsi also found a hidden treasure trove in a cabinet at the offices one day. "By total accident I found a whole bunch of football magazines—there were two great football magazines, *Street and Smith's* and *Football Illustrated*, from the '40s and early '50s," he recalled. "I took them home, and as I was looking at them, there would be a pencil underlining of certain players. Now you know that was Wellington Mara. It couldn't have been anybody else. I know those players from the early '50s. I had their football cards. And, incredibly, the percentage of players that he underlined—people that were nobodies, were not All-Americans—the percentage of those players that made the league just blew me away. I read them all."

With Wellington Mara at the helm, the Giants won six NFL championships (two of them Super Bowls), nine conference championships (including six Eastern Conference titles before the NFL-AFL merger and three NFC championships), and 13 division championships.

Behind the scenes, Wellington and Jack Mara unselfishly helped keep the NFL afloat. By the time of Tim Mara's death in 1959, the

Be Prepared

Ernie Accorsi said he knew that Tom Coughlin, after he was relieved of his duties by the Jacksonville Jaguars, would find a new job. It was his worth ethic and confidence in himself. "He is really a man of faith and into his family, but other than that you can just see that he is all about winning," said Accorsi. "Last year in Indianapolis [at the college combine] he did not have a job. All of the coaches were there, and there were a lot of coaches doing some socializing, too. Tom always caught my eye in the past because he was always at the finish line with a stopwatch and all his papers. Last year he didn't have a team and he was in the same spot. During the breaks after one of the sessions, I said, 'You're incredible! You're still in the same spot, doing the same thing, and you don't have a team.' He said, 'I will, and these players will be in the league, so why wouldn't I be here?' The other thing about him was that he always knew what time mass was, I can tell you that."

Longtime Giants owner Wellington Mara passed away in 2005.

Giants were handsomely profitable. During the early 1960s, although New York was the league's largest television market, the Maras agreed to share overall television revenue equally with smaller-market teams, a strategy that has lifted the NFL to untold economic solidarity.

Through it all, Wellington Mara, a devout Catholic, tried to stay in touch with the loyal fan base, dealing with questions from season-ticket holders and clinging to old-school values in an emerging world of sponsorships, new logos, and promotional pageantry.

In 1967, for example, the Pro Bowl organization in Los Angeles planned to stage a pregame 100-yard race between Giants receiver Homer Jones and the Cowboys' Bob Hayes to determine the fastest player in the NFL—and drum up interest in the game. The winner was to receive $25,000; players generally earned between $10,000 and $15,000 for the entire season. Believing the event would be more of a tawdry spectacle unbefitting the league, Mara asked Jones to withdraw and quietly presented him instead with a $5,000 bonus.

Even during the worst years in franchise history—the 1970s—when the family was feuding over the business and the team suffered, Mara rarely lost his composure. And his patience was certainly tested. On November 19, 1978, when Giants quarterback Joe Pisarcik needed only to take a knee to secure a victory in the waning seconds against the Eagles, he handed the ball off, causing what will forever be known as "the Fumble." Defensive back Herman Edwards grabbed it and raced to a game-winning touchdown.

Three weeks later, during a game against the Cardinals, a fan flew a private plane over Giants Stadium with a streamer reading "15 Years of Lousy Football—We've Had Enough." Although there were about 24,000 empty seats, many of the fans in attendance chanted, "We've had enough!"

Mara got the message, although he perceived it as the wrong one. "People said we were cheap and didn't care if we won, because all our games were sold out," Mara told the *New York Times* years later. "That got under my skin. We weren't cheap. We were just stupid. We made a lot of poor personnel decisions on the football field. That's why we lost."

On the recommendation of then–NFL commissioner Pete Rozelle, Mara hired George Young, formerly an executive with the Colts and the Dolphins, as general manager. The Giants soon put together a string of solid seasons and, under head coach Bill Parcells, won the Super Bowl in 1987.

A Little Perspective

Coaching is hell, except it doesn't last as long, someone said. Coaches are hired, fired, rehired, remaindered, and remanded. It takes perspective when you lose a job, and Jim Fassel received that lesson from his son. "Two years ago on Thanksgiving—that weekend we lost a tough game. I went home and I just didn't want to talk to anyone, I was by myself," he said. "My son John was there, he had flown in for the game, and he said 'Dad, how you doing?' I said, 'I'm not doing very well. I don't think we played well today and I don't really feel like talking about it much.' He said 'Well, let me tell you something. Five years from now, you won't even remember who you played or who you lost to, but I will always remember, for the rest of my life that I was with you on the sideline Thanksgiving weekend.' That meant a lot to me."

"Wellington never told me what to do," Young once said. "But I listened to him because he had all this experience. He was an owner who had directly run a football team. People asked me if I consulted him, and I told them, 'If I lived next to a great big library, I would take advantage of the great, big library.'"

Mara, who was inducted into the Hall of Fame in 1997, was well-liked by the players. He hung with them if they struggled with off-the-field problems. In Lawrence Taylor's own induction speech in Canton, he praised Mara for supporting him during his drug addiction. "He probably cared more about me as a person than he really should have," he said. After the defeat of the Broncos in Super Bowl XXI, Harry Carson, a team captain, impishly edged Mara into the shower in the jubilant locker room—and got away with it.

Wearing a fishing hat and carrying a folding chair even in his eighties, Mara would stop and talk to players during drills, often with his longtime friend Ronnie Barnes alongside. He still cherished that side of the game.

During one long boardroom debate on the complicated plans for renovating or financing a new Giants Stadium, Wellington Mara was silent. He eventually got up, started to leave the meeting, and said, according to his son, John, "I was fine with the Polo Grounds. As far as I'm concerned, we should never have left."

The last Giants game of Mara's life was a come-from-behind 24–23 victory over Denver on a Manning pass to Amani Toomer with five seconds to play. Mara, 89, died of cancer in the final week of October 2005. The team paid one last emotional tribute to Mara that following Sunday at Giants Stadium, ripping the Redskins 36–0.

Tiki Barber ran for 57 yards on the first play of the game, added 59 on another, and totalled 206 for the day in the rout. "The emotion and circumstance of last week, to be able to have my best day, was something I'll never forget," said Barber. "We did what Mr. Mara would have wanted us to do, which was carry on." After a four-yard touchdown in the third, Barber tossed the ball to Tim McDonnell, one of Mara's grandsons, saying, "This one was for the Duke."

Two days earlier, at St. Patrick's Cathedral in Manhattan, an overflow crowd of former players and coaches, league executives, media members, and fans joined the Mara family and friends in his honor.

In a warm, elegant eulogy, John Mara painted a detailed, at times humorous, but indelibly lasting portrait of his father that left the entire cathedral misty-eyed.

"I couldn't help but think he would have been so embarrassed by all this," Mara said. "The police escort, the traffic being stopped, the bagpipes; he would have just shook his head and tried to hide somewhere."

His father always avoided pregame parties or festivities. "For him, he was where he wanted to be, with his players and coaches, but off to the background so as not to interfere," Mara said. "During our road games, he always sat in the press box, never one for a fancy suite or entertaining people during a game, his focus was on the game…. He attended nearly every practice from mini-camp right through the end of the season. It didn't matter if we were 10–2 or 2–10, he was there, wearing that old floppy hat, carrying that ridiculous stool, and usually wearing a shirt or a jacket that was almost as old as he was. Each year our equipment manager would give him the new apparel for the season, and it would always wind up in the same place, stuck in the back of his closet, and out would come the same old and battered outfits. When we changed our logo several years ago back to the traditional lowercase *ny*, he actually started wearing some of the shirts that he had worn the last time we had used that logo more than 25 years before. 'I knew they would come back,' he said."

His ceaseless devotion to the Giants and his family never wavered. Remembering that his grandfather wanted Wellington to go to law school after Fordham, John Mara said that his father pleaded, "'Just give me one year with the team.' My grandfather agreed, and that number turned into 68.... There was a time years ago when he was criticized for loyalty and for it clouding his judgment. 'If that's the worst thing they can say about you,' he would say, 'then you must be doing something right.' I remember going on countless road trips with him over the years, and he would always make it a habit to call a former player or coach in the town that we were playing in. Many of these guys were long forgotten by many of these people, but not by him."

Mara recalled that his parents "went to mass every day, and he made sure that we went on every Sunday and holy day. Long after we were married with children of our own, he would still call to remind us about an upcoming holy day of obligation. Each year at Christmastime, the confession schedule of our parish was hung on the refrigerator door with a little handwritten note: 'No confession, no Santa.' He was married to my mother for more than 51 years, and they had as wonderful a marriage as I have ever seen.... They met of course in church when a woman fainted and they both went to assist her. My father later claimed that the whole thing was staged by my mother's Aunt Lil in order to get his attention. Well, after 51 years of marriage, 11 children, 40 grandchildren, soon to be 42, I would say that she got his attention."

When his parents celebrated their 50th wedding anniversary in St. Patrick's, Mara remembered, "My mother asked him if they could renew their vows. He was very reluctant at first. 'The original ones haven't expired yet, have they?' he said. Of course, he went along with it, but when Cardinal Egan asked him during the ceremony, 'Will you accept children lovingly from God?' The look on his face seemed to say, 'Your eminence, I think that ship sailed a long time ago.'"

Finally, Mara brought his father's career and life full circle.

"'What can you expect from an Irishman named Wellington, whose father was a bookmaker?' A local sportswriter derisively wrote those words about 30 years ago during a time when we were going through some pretty awful seasons," Mara declared.

"My father usually didn't let criticism from the media affect him very much, but those words stung him in a very personal way.... 'I'll tell you what you can expect,' he said at our kickoff luncheon just a few days later. 'You can expect anything he says or writes may be repeated aloud in your own home in front of your own children. You can believe that he was taught to love and respect all mankind, but to fear no man. And you could believe that his abiding ambitions were to pass onto his family the true richness of the inheritance he received from his father, the bookmaker: the knowledge and love and fear of God, and second, to give you a Super Bowl winner.'"

acknowledgments

Having been a New Yorker my entire life and a journalist here for the last 30 or so years, the New York Giants were always threads in the fabric of a multicolored sports dreamcoat. From clipping black-and-white newspaper photographs as a youngster to being locked into radio and TV broadcasts of their Sunday games, I sipped from the Big Blue fountain early.

As a columnist for *Newsday* and a writer for other newspapers, I've covered some of their practices, regular-season and playoff games, and Super Bowls and had the pleasure of interviewing and spending time in the broadcast booth and in studios with former players such as Phil Simms, Pat Summerall, and many others.

A collection like the one you're holding comes from years of notebooks and tapes overflowing with the words and thoughts of numerous players, coaches, front-office personnel, owners, and opponents, and discussions with longtime fans, among them my late father-in-law, Francis "Bud" Durkin, who, although he could have been mistaken for Joe DiMaggio, carried the Giants in his heart.

Thanks to all of the above and to the New York Giants media relations staff who have been courteous and helpful over the years.

This book also draws from numerous sources beyond memory and personal reporting. It includes material from newspaper archives from the *New York Times*, *Newsday*, the *Daily News*, and New Jersey newspapers such as the *Newark Star-Ledger* and also the *Bergen Record*, where I once worked.

It also was supplemented by stories from fine journalists at magazines such as *Sports Illustrated* and magazines devoted to football, as well as videos from NFL Films and reports from giants.com, nfl.com, pro-football-reference.com, and the commemorative book *75 Seasons: The Complete Story of the National Football League*.

And of course, there are many terrific books about the team, too numerous to mention. But a dozen that I recommend and to which I have referred herein include:

The 50 Greatest Plays in New York Giants Football History, by John Maxymuk.

Giants among Men: How Robustelli, Huff, Gifford, and the Giants Made New York a Football Town and Changed the NFL, by Jack Cavanaugh.

The Giants of New York: The History of Professional Football's Most Fabulous Dynasty, by Barry Gottehrer.

GM: The Inside Story of a Dream Job and the Nightmares That Go With It, by Tom Callahan.

The History of the New York Giants, by Michael E. Goodman.

LT: Over the Edge: Tackling Quarterbacks, Drugs, and a World Beyond Football, by Lawrence Taylor, Steve Serby.

The New York Giants: 75 Years of Championship Football, by John Steinbreder.

Once a Giant, Always...My Two Lives with the New York Giants, by Andy Robustelli, Jack Clary.

Stadium Stories: New York Giants, by Michael Eisen.

Tales from the New York Giants Sideline, by Paul Schwartz.

Wellington: The Maras, the Giants, and the City of New York, by Carlo DeVito.

What Giants They Were: New York Giants Greats Talk about Their Teams, Their Coaches, and the Times of Their Lives, by Richard Whittingham.